This book is dedicated to
Vincent Gervasoni
8th June 1921 – 14th August 2005

Rosa's Farm

Country cooking
Rosa Mitchell

MURDOCH BOOKS

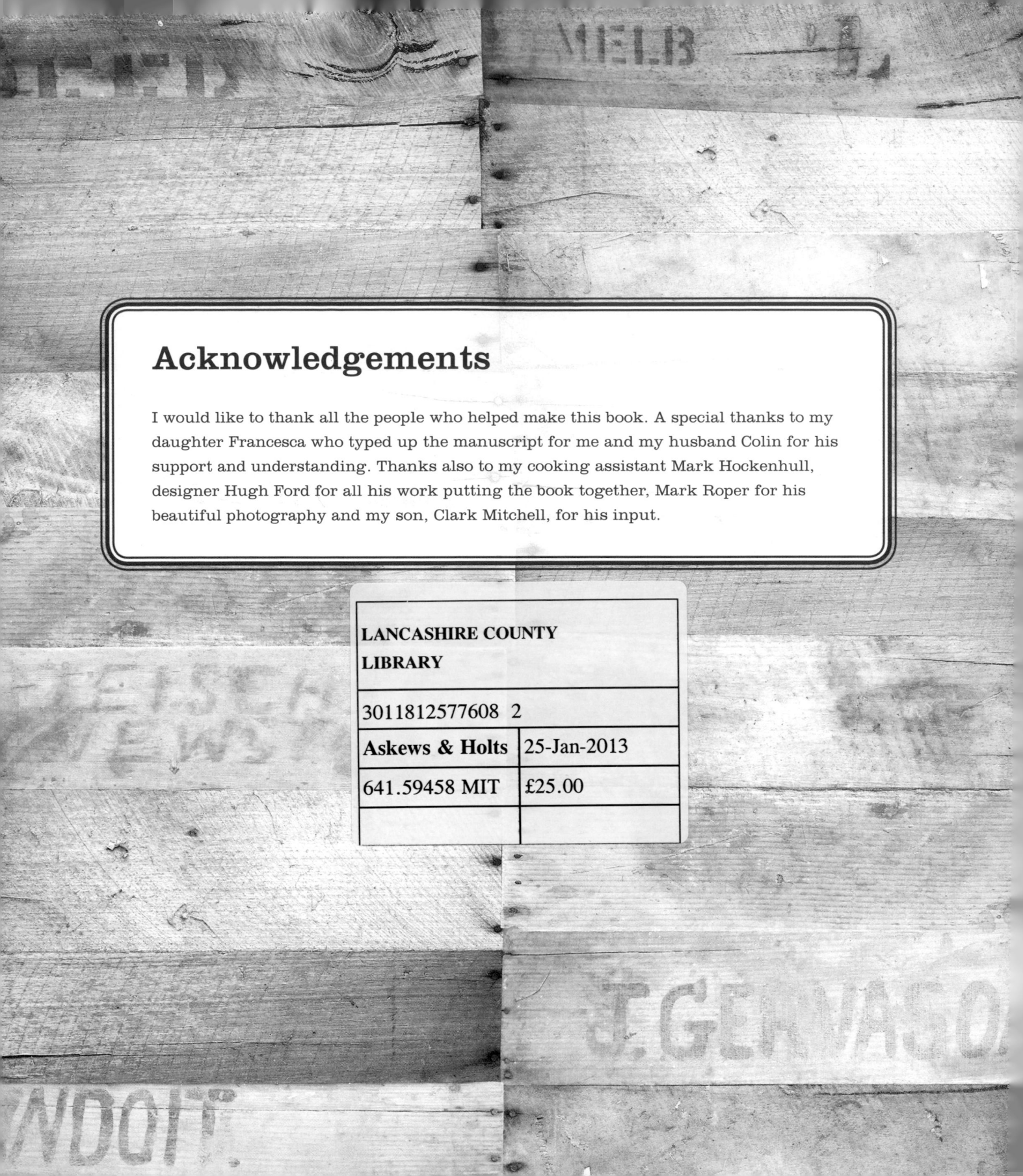

Acknowledgements

I would like to thank all the people who helped make this book. A special thanks to my daughter Francesca who typed up the manuscript for me and my husband Colin for his support and understanding. Thanks also to my cooking assistant Mark Hockenhull, designer Hugh Ford for all his work putting the book together, Mark Roper for his beautiful photography and my son, Clark Mitchell, for his input.

Contents

Introduction

In a landscape dominated by undulating hills and valleys of green bushland laced with running creeks lies the settlement of Yandoit, twenty kilometers north-west of the rural town of Daylesford in Victoria. In 1854, gold was discovered in the nearby Nuggety Gully, which opened the area up to a rush of gold diggers, who in addition to mining, started farming the land, establishing a small community that thrived during the 1860s, only to dwindle once the rush for gold subsided. Even from its earliest beginnings it had a reputation as an Italian enclave — the Gervasoni family being instrumental in creating much of the character surrounding the old stone houses, barns, wells and mines, which even today sparks much interest from historical groups and the National Trusts of Australia.

Of course, in the late eighties, I had never heard of Yandoit. I had been married for a little over ten years and had two small children, Francesca, aged seven and Clark, five. At this stage of my life I was working as a hairdresser in Melbourne. My husband Colin and I had somehow managed to pay off a small inner suburban home and had started thinking of purchasing a weekender out of the city. In my dreams, this was to be a coastal retreat by the sea where I could relax and enjoy the salty air. Colin, on the other hand, had grown up with a family beach house and thought the idea was terribly boring. He was envisioning a place in the country where he could grow grapes, make wine and get his hands dirty. After many discussions we decided on a compromise. We would look in a central Victoria for a comfortable house with a small plot of land that would not be too overwhelming for us to maintain or become a 'rod for our backs' — we were both committed to jobs in the city and the kids had settled into school. We searched for months, but anything we both liked we couldn't afford.

Then, one day Colin came home with an old magazine he'd found in a secondhand shop. It was filled with pictures of beautiful old stone houses situated on rolling green hills and surrounded by orchards and vineyards. It turned out it wasn't far from where we had been looking for real estate. The article mentioned the name of a man who owned several of the buildings. We immediately resolved to find his telephone number — it was a stretch, but perhaps he would like to show us around and maybe even alert us to something that was for sale in the area.

The man was Vincent Gervasoni and unbeknownst to us, he had quite a reputation. I phoned from a nearby town and can remember coming out of the phone box and saying to Colin what an odd conversation it had been, but Vincent had muttered 'If you can be here in ten minutes,

I'll see you'. As we approached his house we saw large signs on the outbuilding 'National Trust, Italian Historical Society and Tourists NOT WELCOME'.

At the top of the driveway waited a tall slim man in his sixties, dressed in overalls, with hands the size of frying pans. He introduced himself as Vince and invited us to enter his home. Despite his wary attitude to strangers, we instantly hit it off. Within minutes, Vince had me attempting to translate an old letter that his relatives had brought over from Italy, while at the same time giving Colin a tour of his 'museum' of original farming implements that had survived over the generations — together we made a good game of guessing what each of the original tools was designed for. As we walked around his property, Vince told many stories of the old days, about his life growing up in the area and the rich Italian heritage that was at the heart of life on the farm (his family heralding from the north of Italy near the Swiss border). Afterwards, we all warmly shook hands and Vince gave me a hug (he was always partial to a hug). As we strolled down the drive towards the car, Vince reverted to his gruff, defensive persona and said, 'What did you come here for anyway?'

I replied that we were looking for something to purchase in the area. Firmly he told us that the area was 'locked up', implying that nothing ever comes up for sale at Yandoit Creek, but to leave our number just in case.

Colin and I couldn't stop talking all the way home. We felt we had met someone special and discovered a place that was different and wonderfully secretive. Two days later there was a short message on our answering machine: 'It's Vince Gervasoni. I've spoken to the woman on the corner. She'll sell.'

Excitedly, I drove up to complete the purchase, not really knowing what I was buying. By the end of the day we were the proud owners of twenty acres of cleared land running up a volcanic hill, a few fruit trees and a dilapidated one-room milking shed. It was almost the exact opposite of my original coastal fantasy, but I loved it. Within weeks the old milking shed was liveable, Colin had planted grapevines, Francesca was enthusiastically embracing nature and Vince had taught Clark to stand at the side of the road, shake his fist and shout 'bloody tourists' at every passing car.

We spent every weekend and holiday at the farm, renovating the shed, planting fruit and olive trees and extending the vineyard by adding five acres of grape vines, including cabernet, cabernet franc and the Italian varietals nebbiolo and arneis, which we started selling to the public in 1994. Vince's family had planted vines on the property in the 1860s, which were productive until he cut them down with his tractor to use the land for grazing. After he saw the successes we were having with our grapes he wanted us to resurrect his shiraz vines. Obviously, when these vines were first planted they were grown without irrigation, which fitted with our philosophy of viticulture (this practice is not common in vineyards today and generally not economically viable). We resolved to rise to the challenge.

Even though our living quarters were quite small, we still managed to entertain and have lots of friends stopping by to visit. We would catch yabbies from the dam, make bullboars (traditional Italian sausages) and buy fresh raspberries from the local berry farm to create lovely meals to share. The pizza oven proved to be an important asset, especially when we needed to feed large groups at harvesting time. We would make tasty pizzas, lasagnas and roasts, sometimes feeding up to sixty people! When my mother came up to visit she would stop off and buy fresh local milk to use to make ricotta and other cheeses in the traditional way. It was during this period that my passion for food and cooking began to shine through.

Our friendship with Vince became stronger. He always seemed to be helping us with something, but because he was such a private person it was hard to repay the favour. Vince's older sister, Rene, lived alone, a short walk down the hill. Each day at midday she would make his lunch and leave his evening meal. They would dine alone. In 1999 Rene passed away and Vince's health started to deteriorate. He had been a cigarette smoker all his life and his shortness of breath was making the big farm chores difficult. One winter weekend we found him in very poor condition with a respiratory infection. We forced him into the car and off to the local hospital. It was the first time he had been to hospital in his life. The doctor felt that Vince needed to be admitted, but Vince refused, saying the dogs and the cows couldn't manage without him. I realised that I would need to become more involved and started to help prepare his daily meals, while Colin tried to help out more (where Vince would let him) on the farm.

I had a lot of fun making single serve size stews and sweet and savoury pies which I would load into Vince's freezer. He would give me kangaroo tails to make up large batches of soup, which I would enthusiastically cook with an Italian twist.

He became a little more confident of our help and with the assistance of his neighbour and cousin, Maurie, we were able to convince him to have short stays in hospital when he was at his lowest. Every week I would drive up the hill past his house to find him standing next to his truck on the roadway. It became a ritual. I would stop and say, 'How are you Vince?' He would reply 'All the better for seeing you.' We would exchange the obligatory cuddle and off I would go. One day as I turned the corner I could see him slumped over the back of the truck. We took him inside, stoked up the fire, made him a sandwich to eat and poured him a glass of wine. He said he felt comfortable. Colin told him he'd be back to 'annoy him' further in the morning. Vince passed away during the night. We knew our lives and the district would never be the same.

Vince owned vast tracts of land and had always felt the responsibility weighed heavily on him to be the custodian of the family farm. As a single man of modest income he had done a great job but unfortunately many of the original buildings had fallen into disrepair — over the span of 150 years it had been hard work to maintain their historic character and charm. The ones that were more important to modern daily life received more attention and money.

There were critics and some speculation on what would become of the property and we were dreading the thought of development. To our surprise, Vince had decided to divide the property and will it to his five adjoining neighbours. Our property increased to 350 acres and we immediately set about restoring the original family home and the stone stables that came with it.

Vince's 1940 Chevrolet truck now has brakes again and the vegetable garden is in full production. Maintaining a sense of historic isolation may be harder to achieve, but I will be holding on tightly to the spirit of Vince and the Gervasoni legacy and fighting change where possible. Will I be gentler on tourists than he? I'll think about it!

Eggs, milk and bread

I like nothing better than visiting the chook pen each morning to collect freshly laid eggs, except perhaps the satisfaction I get from using them to cook a simple, tasty meal. Many years ago I heard someone say that there is no difference between organic free-range eggs and regular eggs, most of which are cage-laid. I couldn't disagree more and think that there is a huge difference in flavour, while the hands-on experience of looking after your own chickens is wonderful for children and grown-ups alike. Home-baked bread is another example of how making your own from scratch is better than store-bought, especially if you have a wood-fired oven. As a child living in Sicily my mother and aunt would bake bread that would stay fresh all week long.

This is a great dish to serve for breakfast, or any time of day really — it is simple, yet hearty. If you like you can chop 3 slices bacon and add to the pan with the onions for extra flavour.

Eggs in tomato

Serves 4

INGREDIENTS

60 ml (2 fl oz/¼ cup)
    olive oil
½ onion, diced
400 g (14 oz) tin Italian
    chopped tomatoes
    or 6–8 ripe tomatoes,
    chopped
4 organic or free-range eggs
chilli flakes (optional),
    to serve

METHOD

Heat the olive oil in a large non-stick frying pan over medium heat. Add the onion and cook until the onion is soft and translucent, then add the tomatoes and cook gently for about 15 minutes, stirring occasionally; season with salt and pepper, to taste.

When the tomatoes are cooked, spread them evenly in the base of the pan and gently break the eggs over the top so that they are spread evenly in the pan. Season again, and cook gently until the eggs have set to your liking. If you prefer, you can break the eggs in the pan, stirring gently to scramble them. Sprinkle over the chilli flakes, if using, and serve over toasted bread.

Sicilian toast

Serves 4

METHOD

In a mixing bowl, beat the eggs, then add the parmesan and parsley and stir to combine. Season with salt and pepper, to taste. Set aside.

Heat the olive oil in a large non-stick frying pan over medium heat. Working with one piece of bread at a time, dip a slice of bread into the egg mixture for 30 seconds, then add to the pan and cook for 1 minute on each side, or until golden. Remove to a plate while cooking the remainder. Sprinkle with a little salt and pepper and serve hot or warm.

INGREDIENTS

4 organic or free-range eggs

35 g (1¼ oz/¼ cup) finely grated parmesan cheese

2 tablespoons finely chopped flat-leaf (Italian) parsley

125 ml (4 fl oz/½ cup) olive oil

4–6 slices good-quality Italian-style white bread

You can use either pitted or whole olives in this recipe to good effect, but I prefer whole olives, as I find the flavour is always better, although it is a bit more fiddly, as you will need to eat around the stones.

Fried eggs with black olives

Serves 4

INGREDIENTS

60 ml (2 fl oz/¼ cup)
   olive oil
1 teaspoon garlic in oil
   (page 213)
16 black olives
4 organic or free-range eggs

METHOD

Heat the olive oil in a large non-stick frying pan over medium heat. Add the garlic and let brown slightly. Add the olives, toss for a few seconds, then crack the eggs into the pan and fry until the eggs are set to your liking. Serve with toasted bread or just good fresh crusty bread, for dipping.

This simple salad really needs home-grown or good-quality tomatoes.
It is perfect for serving on a summer's day. You can serve it with a few
slices of prosciutto or with a beautiful buffalo mozzarella cheese.

Panzanella

Serves 6

INGREDIENTS

3 slices good-quality
   Italian-style white bread
1 kg (2 lb 4 oz) ripe
      tomatoes or use
      a mixture of heirloom
      tomatoes
1 onion, thinly sliced
2 tablespoons capers, rinsed
   and squeezed dry
1 celery heart, thinly sliced
125 ml (4 fl oz/½ cup) olive
      oil
2 tablespoons red wine
      vinegar
1 handful basil, leaves
      picked

METHOD

Toast the slices of bread until crunchy, then allow to cool.
Cut into small cubes and place in a mixing bowl.

Cut the tomatoes into small pieces and place in the
bowl with the bread. Add the onion, capers and celery
and stir to combine. Pour in the combined oil and vinegar
and mix well to coat all of the ingredients; season with
salt and pepper, to taste.

Leave the salad to rest for about 30 minutes before
serving to give the juices a chance to soak into the bread.
Just before serving, add the basil leaves, toss to combine
and serve at room temperature.

Orecchiette with asparagus and ricotta

Serves 4–6

METHOD

Bring a large saucepan of salted water to the boil.
Blanch the asparagus in the boiling water for 1 minute
and set aside. Reserve the water to cook the pasta in.

Heat 60 ml (2 fl oz/¼ cup) of the olive oil in a large
frying pan over medium heat. Add the breadcrumbs and
garlic and toss in the pan until they turn golden. Remove
to a bowl, and when cool, add the parmesan and parsley
and mix well; season with salt and pepper, to taste.

Bring the reserved saucepan of water to the boil and
cook the orecchiette according to the packet directions.
Drain well.

Add the remaining oil to the pan and stir-fry the
asparagus over medium heat for about 5 minutes, or
until it starts to colour. Add the pasta and toss well to
combine, seasoning, to taste. Crumble the ricotta into
the pasta and lightly mix it through. Divide the pasta
between serving bowls and sprinkle the breadcrumb
mixture over the top before serving.

NOTE: You can add 2–3 anchovies or 1 teaspoon
chilli flakes to this dish when you are pan-frying
the asparagus, if you like.

INGREDIENTS

2–3 bunches asparagus,
   trimmed and sliced on
   the diagonal into 3–4 cm
   (1¼–1½ inch) lengths
125 ml (4 fl oz/½ cup) olive
   oil
50 g (1¾ oz/¾ cup) fresh
   white breadcrumbs
1 teaspoon garlic in oil
   (page 213)
35 g (1¼ oz/¼ cup) finely
   grated parmesan cheese
3 tablespoons finely chopped
   flat-leaf (Italian) parsley
500 g (1 lb 2 oz) orecchiette
   pasta
200 g (7 oz) fresh ricotta
   cheese

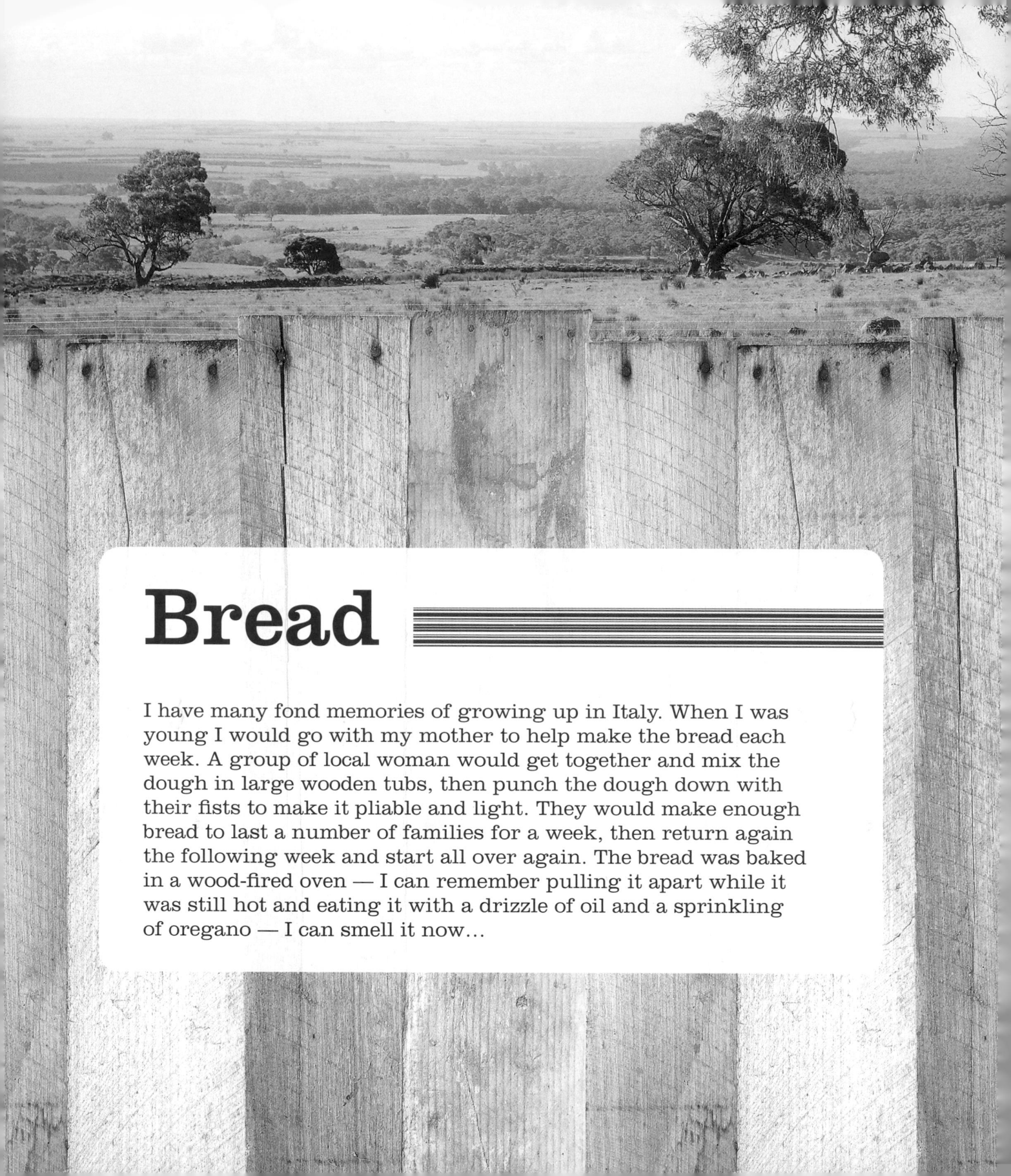

Bread

I have many fond memories of growing up in Italy. When I was young I would go with my mother to help make the bread each week. A group of local woman would get together and mix the dough in large wooden tubs, then punch the dough down with their fists to make it pliable and light. They would make enough bread to last a number of families for a week, then return again the following week and start all over again. The bread was baked in a wood-fired oven — I can remember pulling it apart while it was still hot and eating it with a drizzle of oil and a sprinkling of oregano — I can smell it now...

This is a good way to use a leftover loaf of bread which has gone stale. The amounts included below are a guide only — the amounts you use will depend on the size and type of bread and your own palate. You can also add thin slices of fresh tomato — yum!

Seasoned hot bread

Serves 6–8

METHOD

Preheat the oven to 160°C (315°F/Gas 2–3). Place the bread on an oven tray and cook for 20 minutes. Remove from the oven and while still hot, slice the loaf in half horizontally.

Sprinkle both halves generously with the olive oil, oregano, garlic and chilli, if using, then season with salt and pepper, to taste. Replace the bread top, cut into slices widthways and serve hot.

INGREDIENTS

1 loaf good-quality Italian-style bread, such as ciabatta or pagnotta
125 ml (4 fl oz/½ cup) good-quality olive oil
1 tablespoon dried oregano
2 teaspoons garlic in oil (page 213)
1–2 teaspoons chilli flakes (optional)

Dried ricotta is a delicious alternative to grated parmesan cheese for serving over pastas, soups and salads. If you only bake it for two nights it is also lovely to eat as a simple cheese with bread. When buying ricotta, you need to purchase from the large 3–4 kg (6 lb 12 oz–9 lb) rounds sold in good delicatessens.

Dried ricotta cheese

Makes 2 nice big wedges

INGREDIENTS

1.5 kg (3 lb 5 oz) fresh
   ricotta cheese
65 g (2½ oz/½ cup) salt

METHOD

Preheat the oven to the lowest possible setting. Cut the ricotta in half, place on a baking tray lined with baking paper, then rub the salt all over to coat. Place in the oven and leave overnight, or at least 12 hours. Turn the ricotta over and cook for a further 12 hours, then repeat a further two times, or until the ricotta is firm to the touch. Between cooking, place the ricotta outside in the sun or on an open airy bench. The cooking time will vary depending on the oven.

Dried ricotta can be stored in the refrigerator wrapped in foil or muslin (cheesecloth) — it will keep for up to 2 months.

NOTE: You can also dry fresh ricotta out in the hot sun, but make sure it is brought in every night. Finish off in the oven for a little colour.

Italians don't really have dessert, as such, after a meal — it's usually enough just to finish with a little fruit or a small sweet offering. This dish is perfect for sharing after a meal with an espresso, then you can eat as much or as little as you like.

Fried milk

Serves 6–8

CREAM

5 egg yolks

125 g (4½ oz) caster (superfine) sugar, plus extra for dusting

50 g (1¾ oz) cornflour (cornstarch)

500 ml (17 fl oz/2 cups) milk

3–4 drops natural vanilla extract

1 strip lemon zest

100 g (3½ oz/⅔ cup) plain (all-purpose) flour

2 free-range eggs, lightly beaten

200 g (7 oz/1¾ cups) dried breadcrumbs

vegetable oil, for frying

2 teaspoons ground cinnamon

METHOD

In a bowl, beat the egg yolks with the sugar until well combined. Add the cornflour, a little at a time, until well incorporated, then stir in the milk and vanilla extract. Transfer to a saucepan, add the lemon zest, and place over low heat. Bring the mixture to a gentle boil, then remove from the heat, take out the lemon peel, and pour the cream into a 23 x 29 cm (9 x 11½ inch) lamington tin lined with baking paper. Cool to room temperature and refrigerate for at least 8 hours, or overnight.

Cut the cold cream into 4 cm (1½ inch) squares. Put the flour, eggs and breadcrumbs in separate bowls.

Heat about 1 cm (½ inch) vegetable oil in a shallow frying pan over medium heat. Working in small batches, dip the squares first into the flour to dust, then into the egg, then roll in the breadcrumbs to coat, shaking off any excess. Repeat again with the remaining squares, egg and breadcrumbs. When the oil is hot, cook the squares until golden on the underside, then turn and cook the other side until golden. Remove from the oil and drain on paper towel.

In a shallow bowl, combine the extra caster sugar and cinnamon. Dip the warm fried milk squares into the sugar mixture to lightly coat and serve while still warm.

Clark is my son who is also a chef. He loves making ice cream and the ice cream machine we bought has been the best investment we have ever made for him as it is in constant use. He has impressed everyone with the flavour combinations he has come up with — this is one of my favourites.

Clark's cinnamon and marsala ice cream

Makes 2 litres (70 fl oz)

METHOD

Put the milk, cream, ground cinnamon, cinnamon stick, and the vanilla seeds and pod into a large saucepan over medium heat. Bring to the boil, then remove from the heat immediately and set aside to cool to room temperature. Discard the cinnamon stick and vanilla pod.

Put the egg yolks and Marsala in the bowl of an electric mixer fitted with a whisk attachment and whisk until white, thick and fluffy.

Put the caster sugar and 150 ml (5 fl oz) water into a separate saucepan and heat to 118°C (244°F) — test this using a kitchen thermometer. Once the sugar reaches the correct temperature, slowly pour into the egg mixture, whisking continuously until all of the sugar syrup is incorporated, then increase the speed and whisk until the mixture is completely cool — this takes quite a while so be patient.

Add the milk mixture to the bowl and whisk together to combine. Place in the refrigerator to cool down. When the mixture is cold, transfer to an ice-cream machine and freeze according to the manufacturer's instructions.

Serve the ice cream on its own or try it with the pears baked with dates, Marsala and honey on page 184.

INGREDIENTS

500 ml (17 fl oz/2 cups) milk

500 ml (17 fl oz/2 cups) pouring (whipping) cream

3 tablespoons ground cinnamon

1 cinnamon stick

1 vanilla bean, split lengthways and seeds scraped

10 egg yolks

25 ml (1 fl oz) Marsala

300 g (10½ oz/1⅓ cups) caster (superfine) sugar

This is my *zia's* (auntie's) recipe. You can make this in a round bowl or rectangular dish. The shape is not that important — it will just mean you will have more or less layers.

Zuppa inglese (Italian trifle)

Serves 6–8

CUSTARD

1 litre (35 fl oz/4 cups) milk

220 g (7¾ oz/1 cup) sugar

½ teaspoon finely grated lemon zest

2 strips lemon zest

2 egg yolks, beaten with 1 tablespoon milk

60 g (2¼ oz/½ cup) cornflour (cornstarch), mixed with 125 ml (4 fl oz/½ cup) milk to form a smooth paste

125 ml (4 fl oz/½ cup) very strong Italian coffee

250 ml (9 fl oz/1 cup) Marsala

500 g (1 lb 2 oz) Savoiardi (sponge finger) biscuits

2 tablespoons dark cocoa powder

3–4 tablespoons flaked almonds, lightly toasted

METHOD

To make the custard, put the milk, sugar, lemon zest and strips, and the egg yolks into a saucepan over medium heat to warm slightly. Add the cornflour mixture, reduce the heat to medium–low, and stir constantly until the custard thickens and starts to boil — this takes about 15 minutes. Remove from the heat and set aside to cool for 30 minutes.

In a separate bowl, mix together the coffee and Marsala. Place a little of the custard in a 2.5 litre (87 fl oz) capacity serving bowl or rectangular dish. Dip the biscuits quickly into the coffee mixture to coat, then arrange over the top of the custard to make an even layer. Add another layer of custard to cover the biscuits, and continue layering this way, finishing with a layer of custard to fill the dish, or until all of the biscuits and custard have been used. Refrigerate for at least 4 hours to set.

Just before you are ready to serve, dust the top of the trifle with cocoa and sprinkle over the flaked almonds.

From the garden

The thing I remember most about my grandfather was his huge vegetable garden and the time he spent tending to it. Soon after arriving in Australia he became almost completely self-sufficient, filling his small city plot with asparagus and broad beans, eggplants and zucchini, chicory and other leafy greens that were hard to find in shops at the time. His dedication and perseverance sparked a lifelong interest for me and I take much pleasure in growing my own vegetables to cook with and to share with family and friends. Vince had a similar interest in his vegetable patch on the farm, although like many remote landholders, his was also motivated by necessity. You could always find a vine of ox heart tomatoes growing large in his garden, as well as horseradish. Apart from the obvious benefits of getting cheap quality vegetables, enjoying the variation of produce available each season is a blessing and a joy.

This is a lovely dish that can be served hot or cold and makes a great accompaniment to roast meats or as a base for a frittata.

Chicory and potato

Serves 6 as a side

INGREDIENTS

2–3 nicola potatoes, peeled, halved and thinly sliced

2 bunches chicory, rinsed, drained and chopped into 5 cm (2 inch) lengths

60 ml (2 fl oz/¼ cup) olive oil

1 small white onion, thinly sliced

1 tablespoon garlic in oil (page 213)

METHOD

Cook the potato in a saucepan of boiling water until just tender. Remove with a slotted spoon, drain and set aside. In the same water, cook the chicory for about 5–10 minutes, or until tender — to test this, check the thickest part of the chicory, it should be soft but firm. Drain well and set aside.

Heat the olive oil in a large frying pan over medium heat. Add the onion and cook for about 5 minutes, or until it turns golden. Add the potato, toss with the onions and season with salt and pepper. Add the chicory and garlic, mix well, and cook for about 10 minutes, or until the chicory starts to caramelise slightly. Season, to taste, before serving.

It is always a pleasure to be able to walk into your vegetable garden to pick fresh corn that can then be stripped, cooked and eaten straight away. When my husband lived in the United States he was taught to cook whole corn cobs by boiling them in water with a tablespoon of brown sugar and half a cup of milk — which is a terrific way to enjoy them.

Corn and pancetta

Serves 6

METHOD

Using a sharp knife, cut the corn from the cobs.

Heat the olive oil in a large frying pan over medium heat. Add the pancetta and cook for about 2–3 minutes, then add the corn and garlic and season with salt and pepper, to taste. Reduce the heat to low and cook for about 10–15 minutes, stirring constantly until the corn starts to turn golden. Be careful as the corn may 'pop' occasionally.

This dish is a great addition to a breakfast plate served with poached eggs and tomatoes.

NOTE: Alternatively, you can allow the mixture to cool and make some tasty fritters. Add to a bowl with some finely chopped parsley, about 70 g (2½ oz/½ cup) finely grated parmesan cheese, 150 g (5½ oz/1 cup) self-raising flour and 2 eggs and stir well to combine. Cook spoonfuls of the mixture in a non-stick frying pan with a little olive oil — they should be cooked through and golden on both sides when done.

INGREDIENTS

6 corn cobs, husks removed

80 ml (2½ fl oz/⅓ cup) olive oil

50 g (1¾ oz/⅓ cup) finely chopped pancetta or bacon

1 tablespoon garlic in oil (page 213)

If picking zucchini (courgette) flowers from the garden choose the males, which have thin, long stems and come to full maturity in the summer months. This basic recipe makes a lovely base for a frittata (see page 153) — you will only need to use half of the zucchini mixture.

Pan-fried zucchini and zucchini flowers

Serves 6 as a side

INGREDIENTS

1 handful of zucchini (courgette) flowers
6 young or 4 large zucchinis (courgettes)
125 ml (4 fl oz/½ cup) olive oil
1 onion, thinly sliced

METHOD

Wash the zucchini flowers gently and drain well. Trim the zucchini, cut in half horizontally and then cut into 1 cm (½ inch) pieces.

Heat the olive oil in a deep frying pan over medium heat. Add the onion and cook for about 5 minutes, then add the zucchini and cook for 10 minutes, stirring occasionally until just tender. Add the zucchini flowers and reduce the heat to low. Season with salt and pepper and cook slowly until the zucchini start to break up and become quite soft — a little water may be added if they start to stick. Remove from the heat and serve hot — this dish goes well with most meat dishes.

NOTE: You can also create a lovely soup from this dish. Once it is cooked, add enough water to cover the zucchini and bring to the boil. Add about 1 cup of your favourite small pasta and cook until al dente, then adjust the seasoning as needed, divide between serving bowls and serve with some grated parmesan cheese on top.

You can make this recipe using zucchini (courgettes) and substitute the basil for mint leaves. Any leftovers can be chopped up and used to make a delicious pasta sauce.

Slow-cooked eggplant

Serves 6 as a side

METHOD

Preheat the oven to 180°C (350°F/Gas 4).

Chop off about 2 cm (¾ inch) from the narrow end of each eggplant. Use a small sharp knife to make a small hole in the middle of the eggplant by rotating the knife, scraping out the middle and leaving the sides intact to prevent the walls from collapsing during cooking.

In a bowl, combine the basil, parmesan, garlic and 60 ml (2 fl oz/¼ cup) of the olive oil. Season with salt and pepper, then place a little stuffing into the hole in each eggplant, pushing down firmly and using a little of the scooped out eggplant to plug the hole at the top to help keep the filling in.

Place the remaining oil in a frying pan over medium heat. Add the eggplants and turn to brown on all sides, then remove to a baking tray.

To make the tomato sauce, add the onion to the same pan and cook for 10 minutes, or until golden. Add the tomatoes, season with salt and pepper, and cook for a further 10 minutes. Pour the tomato sauce over the eggplant in the tray and add 250 ml (9 fl oz/1 cup) water. Cover with a sheet of baking paper and then seal the tray with a layer of foil. Cook in the oven for 40 minutes, or until a skewer can be easily inserted through the eggplant. Serve with the extra parmesan cheese on top.

INGREDIENTS

6 very small or thin long eggplants (aubergines)
½ bunch basil, leaves picked and finely chopped
35 g (1¼ oz/¼ cup) finely grated parmesan cheese, plus extra, to serve
½ teaspoon finely chopped garlic
185 ml (6 fl oz/¾ cup) olive oil

TOMATO SAUCE

1 small onion, finely diced
1 x 400 g (14 oz) tin Italian chopped tomatoes, puréed

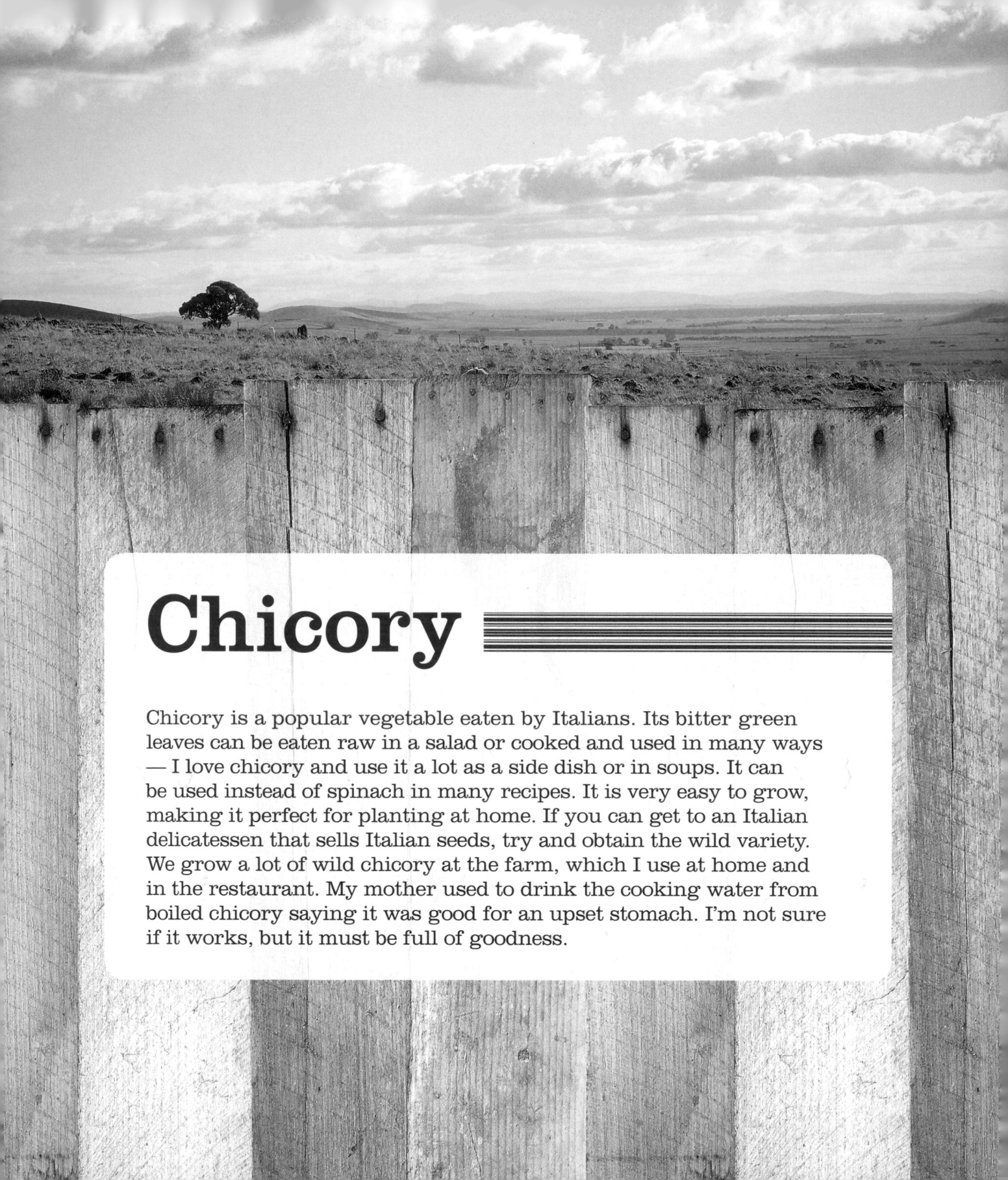

Chicory

Chicory is a popular vegetable eaten by Italians. Its bitter green leaves can be eaten raw in a salad or cooked and used in many ways — I love chicory and use it a lot as a side dish or in soups. It can be used instead of spinach in many recipes. It is very easy to grow, making it perfect for planting at home. If you can get to an Italian delicatessen that sells Italian seeds, try and obtain the wild variety. We grow a lot of wild chicory at the farm, which I use at home and in the restaurant. My mother used to drink the cooking water from boiled chicory saying it was good for an upset stomach. I'm not sure if it works, but it must be full of goodness.

This is a great vegetable accompaniment, providing a burst of fresh green flavours, to serve with any meat dish, especially pork. It makes a nice change from the oft used spinach, broccoli or green bean side dishes that many people include in their weeknight meals.

Pan-fried chicory with garlic

Serves 6 as a side

METHOD

Cook the chicory in a saucepan of salted boiling water for about 5–10 minutes, then drain well.

Heat the olive oil in a frying pan over medium heat. Add the garlic and cook for about 30 seconds, then add the chicory and season with salt and pepper, to taste. Increase the heat to high and cook for about 10 minutes, stirring constantly, or until tender. Serve hot.

INGREDIENTS

1 bunch chicory, rinsed, drained and chopped into 5 cm (2 inch) lengths

80 ml (2½ fl oz/⅓ cup) olive oil

1 teaspoon finely chopped garlic

Stuffed fennel

Serves 6

INGREDIENTS

3 large fennel bulbs
60 ml (2 fl oz/¼ cup) olive oil
1 onion, diced
1 garlic clove, finely
    chopped
250 g (9 oz) lean minced
    (ground) pork
¼ teaspoon fennel seeds
45 g (1½ oz/¾ cup) fresh
    white breadcrumbs
2 tablespoons finely chopped
    parsley
50 g (1¾ oz/½ cup) finely
    grated parmesan cheese

TOMATO SAUCE

60 ml (2 fl oz/¼ cup) olive oil
1 garlic clove, finely
    chopped
1 x 400 g (14 oz) tin
    Italian chopped tomatoes

METHOD

Remove the outer leaves of the fennel, trim both ends and cut in half, reserving the green fronds. Blanch the fennel in a saucepan of salted boiling water for 10–15 minutes, or until they can be skewered easily — don't overcook. Drain well and when cool enough to handle, use a sharp knife to cut a hollow in the centre of each for the filling. Reserve the flesh and chop it very finely.

To make the filling, heat the olive oil in a large frying pan over medium heat. Add the onion and cook for 2–3 minutes, then add the garlic and pork; season with salt, pepper and fennel seeds. Cook for 10–15 minutes, or until the meat is brown, breaking up any large lumps with a fork. Remove to a large bowl and allow to cool for about 30 minutes, then add the breadcrumbs, parsley, parmesan, the reserved chopped fennel and the fennel fronds. Mix well and adjust the seasoning as needed. Divide the filling mixture evenly between each fennel, pressing firmly to fill each hollow.

Preheat the oven to 180ºC (350ºF/Gas 4). To make the tomato sauce, heat the olive oil in a frying pan over medium heat. Add the garlic and cook for about 30 seconds, then add the tomatoes and 250 ml (9 fl oz/1 cup) water. Season with salt and pepper and cook for a further 15 minutes.

Pour the tomato sauce evenly into a baking tray and place the fennel on top. Cover with a layer of foil and bake in the oven for 1 hour, or until soft — you can test this with a skewer. Serve with a green salad or with the pan-fried chicory and garlic on page 49.

NOTE: You can make a vegetarian version of this dish by omitting the minced pork and using 2–3 extra fennel instead. You will need to finely dice the flesh and cook in place of the pork.

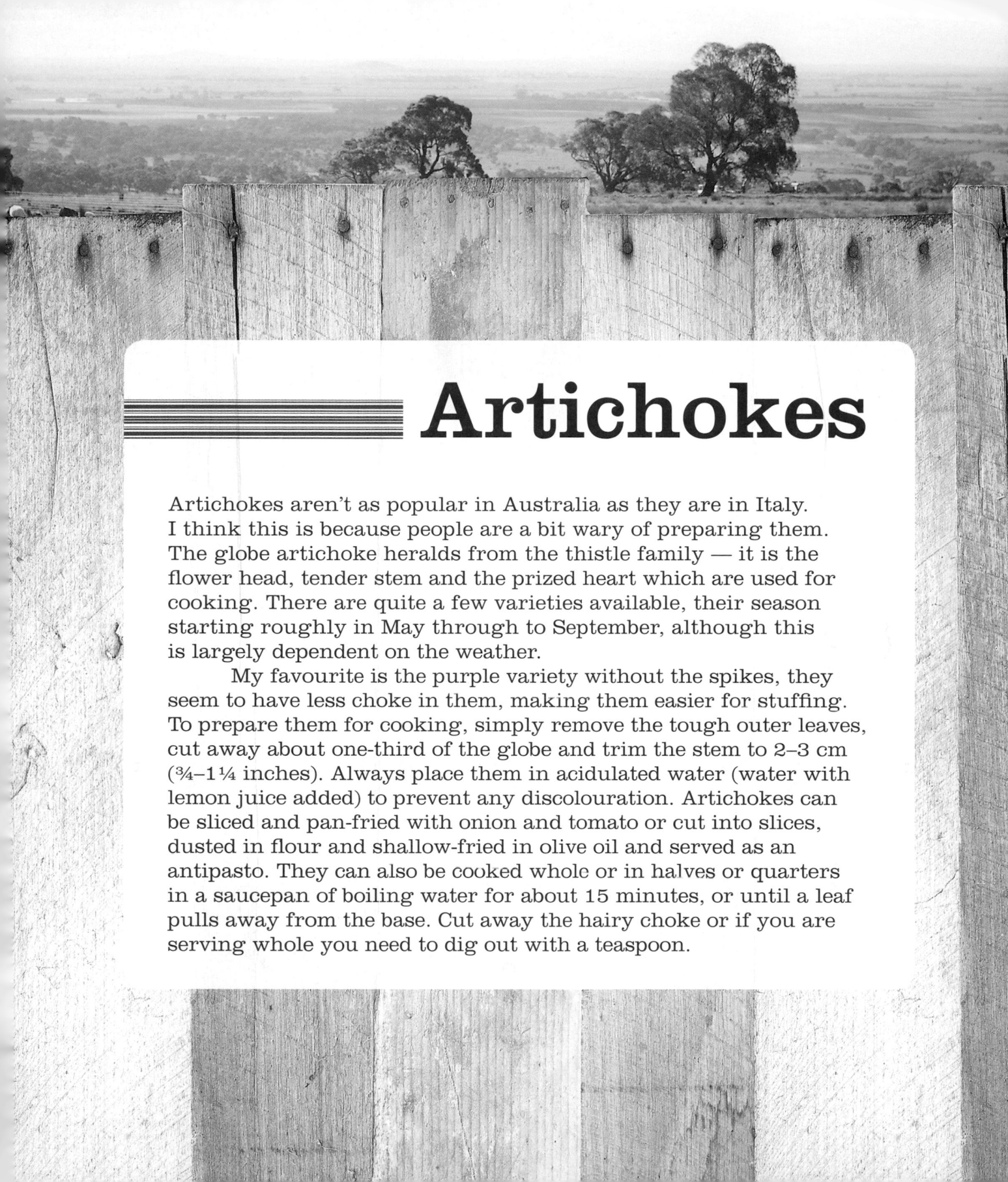

Artichokes

Artichokes aren't as popular in Australia as they are in Italy. I think this is because people are a bit wary of preparing them. The globe artichoke heralds from the thistle family — it is the flower head, tender stem and the prized heart which are used for cooking. There are quite a few varieties available, their season starting roughly in May through to September, although this is largely dependent on the weather.

My favourite is the purple variety without the spikes, they seem to have less choke in them, making them easier for stuffing. To prepare them for cooking, simply remove the tough outer leaves, cut away about one-third of the globe and trim the stem to 2–3 cm (¾–1¼ inches). Always place them in acidulated water (water with lemon juice added) to prevent any discolouration. Artichokes can be sliced and pan-fried with onion and tomato or cut into slices, dusted in flour and shallow-fried in olive oil and served as an antipasto. They can also be cooked whole or in halves or quarters in a saucepan of boiling water for about 15 minutes, or until a leaf pulls away from the base. Cut away the hairy choke or if you are serving whole you need to dig out with a teaspoon.

I first tasted this beautiful dish thirty years ago. Soon after Colin and I were married, we visited my aunt and uncle who live in the hills outside of Rome. My Aunt Santa is the most amazing cook and on one particular night we dined on pigeon and artichokes cooked in the open air over the embers from vine cuttings. If you are unable to make an open fire, you can cook them in a very hot oven or a wood-fired oven instead.

Artichokes cooked in vine embers

Serves 6

INGREDIENTS

vine cuttings, for burning
12 fresh young artichokes
juice of 2 lemons
½ bunch parsley, leaves finely chopped
2 tablespoons chopped fresh mint
2 tablespoons garlic in oil (page 213)
250 ml (9 fl oz/1 cup) extra virgin olive oil

METHOD

Make a fire with the vine cuttings; when there are no flames left but lots of red embers it is ready for the artichokes.

Trim the bottom of the artichokes and cut about 2–3 cm (¾–1¼ inches) from the tops of the artichokes to give you a flat surface. Place into a bowl of water with the lemon juice to stop them from turning brown.

In a bowl, mix together the parsley, mint, garlic and olive oil and season with salt and pepper.

When you are ready to start cooking, take the artichokes out of the water and place them, cut side down, on a work surface. Use your hand to rock them back and forward to open up the leaves a little. Spoon a little of the parsley mixture evenly into the artichoke leaves (not too much), then place the artichokes into the embers, leaving about 4 cm (1½ inches) above the embers — use good gloves and long tongs and be careful as it will be very hot. Cook for about 45 minutes–1 hour. They will char on the outside but you want to eat the smokey heart in the centre — the cooking time will depend on the heat of the fire. The artichokes will look black on the outside but the inside will be soft and they should have a beautiful herb and garlic smell.

You can use any type of pasta for this dish. If you like chilli you can add about 1 teaspoon of chilli flakes to the eggplant pesto with the seasoning.

Eggplant pesto

Serves 4–6

METHOD

Put the garlic and 125 ml (4 fl oz/½ cup) olive oil in a bowl, cover, and leave to stand overnight to allow the garlic to infuse the oil.

Cut each eggplant into about five slices and then dice. Sprinkle over enough salt to lightly cover and leave to stand for about 1 hour — this helps to remove any bitterness. When ready, place on a clean tea towel (dish cloth) to absorb any liquid and pat dry.

Heat about 125 ml (4 fl oz/½ cup) of the olive oil in a large frying pan over medium heat. Add the eggplant in batches, and cook for about 8 minutes, stirring occasionally, until soft and golden. Use a slotted spoon to remove to a plate while cooking the remainder — you may need to add the remaining oil. Once all the eggplant is cooked, set aside to cool.

Transfer the eggplant to a food processor. Strain the oil from the garlic, discarding the garlic, and add the oil to the food processor with the basil. Process to make a purée — you want the mixture to be wet; add extra oil if it is too dry. Place in a bowl and season with salt and pepper, to taste.

Cook the pasta in a saucepan of boiling water according to the packet instructions. Drain well and return to the pan, then stir through the eggplant pesto.

To serve, divide between serving bowls and sprinkle the parmesan cheese or salted dried ricotta over the top.

INGREDIENTS

4 garlic cloves, crushed
330 ml (12 fl oz/1⅓ cups)
 olive oil
3 eggplants (aubergines)
1 bunch basil, leaves picked
500 g (1 lb 2 oz) dried pasta
grated parmesan cheese or
 salted dried ricotta
 (page 28), to serve

Celery, radish and pecorino salad

Serves 6

INGREDIENTS

1 head celery

1 bunch radishes

40 g (1½ oz/½ cup) shaved
pecorino or parmesan
cheese

DRESSING

2 tablespoons red wine
vinegar or juice of
2 lemons

60 ml (2 fl oz/¼ cup) olive
oil

METHOD

Remove the outer sticks of celery — these can be used for a soup or a slow braise. Rinse and dry the centre sticks, the heart and the tender young leaves, then drain well. Slice into small pieces. Wash the radishes well, trimming off the ends, then thinly slice. Place the celery and radishes into a serving bowl.

To make the dressing, combine the red wine vinegar and olive oil in a bowl and season with salt and pepper, to taste. Pour over the celery and radish and toss well to combine, then sprinkle over the shaved pecorino.

NOTE: Instead of pecorino, you can add some crispy pancetta, prosciutto or bacon to this salad. Simply place 4 slices pancetta on a baking tray and cook in 200°C (400°F/Gas 6) oven for 5 minutes, turning once, until crispy. Allow to cool slightly, then crumble over the salad before serving.

Pumpkin, barley and chicory soup

Serves 6

INGREDIENTS

80 ml (2½ fl oz/⅓ cup)
  olive oil
1 brown onion, diced
500 g (1 lb 2 oz/3⅓ cups)
  peeled and cubed
  jap (kent) pumpkin
  (winter squash)
200 g (7 oz/1 cup) pearl
  barley
1 sprig of sage
2 litres (70 fl oz/8 cups)
  chicken stock (page 112)
2 bunches chicory, rinsed,
  drained and thinly sliced

METHOD

Heat the olive oil in a large saucepan over medium heat. Add the onion and cook for about 5 minutes. Add the pumpkin and cook for about 10 minutes — if it starts to stick to the pan, add a little water. Add the barley and mix well for about 1 minute, then add the sage and stock, season with salt and pepper, and simmer over gentle heat for about 40 minutes, or until the barley is tender. Add the chicory and cook for a further 20 minutes, or until the chicory is tender. Divide between serving bowls and serve hot.

NOTE: If chicory is unavailable you can use spinach or silverbeet instead. If using spinach, add during the last 5 minutes of cooking.

Farro is a wholesome grain that was commonly used by the ancient Romans. It was used to make bread and pasta and is available from good delicatessens and speciality food stores. If unavailable, you can use the same quantity of barley instead.

Farro, lentil and vegetable soup

Serves 8

METHOD

Heat the oil in a large saucepan over medium heat. Add the onion, carrot, celery and cabbage and cook for about 10 minutes, stirring occasionally until softened. Add the tomatoes, farro and lentils and cook for a further 5 minutes, stirring occasionally so it doesn't stick to the base of the pan.

Add about 2 litres (70 fl oz/8 cups) water to the pan, then reduce the heat to low and cook gently for about 1½–2 hours, stirring occasionally. You can add more water if desired, it depends on if you want a thick or thinner soup. When the farro and lentils are tender the soup is done. Season with salt and pepper, divide between serving bowls and serve hot.

INGREDIENTS

60 ml (2 fl oz/¼ cup) olive oil

2 brown onions, diced

2 carrots, finely chopped

4 celery sticks, finely chopped

¼ head cabbage, shredded

1 x 400 g (14 oz) tin Italian chopped tomatoes

200 g (7 oz/1 cup) farro

200 g (7 oz/1 cup) red or brown lentils

Pan-fried artichokes

METHOD

Remove the tough outer leaves of the artichokes and trim the stems (in my family we peel and add the stems to the dish — cut them in half lengthways and then into small pieces). You will be left with the lighter coloured and tender heart of the artichoke. Place in a bowl of water with the lemon juice — this will prevent them from turning brown. Just before you start cooking, drain them well and thinly slice, removing the hairy chokes.

Heat the olive oil in a large frying pan over medium heat. Add the anchovies and cook for about 30 seconds, then add the garlic and artichokes. Reduce the heat to low, cover, and cook for about 15–20 minutes, or until the artichokes start to soften and turn golden — you may need to add a little water if it is getting dry.

When the artichokes are cooked, increase the heat to medium, add the parsley and breadcrumbs, toss to combine, and cook for a further 3 minutes. Season well with salt and pepper, then remove from the heat. Transfer to a serving bowl and sprinkle over the parmesan cheese before serving.

INGREDIENTS

6 artichokes
juice of 2 lemons
125 ml (4 fl oz/½ cup)
    olive oil
4 anchovies
1 teaspoon garlic in oil
    (page 213)
2 tablespoons finely
    chopped parsley
30 g (1 oz/½ cup) fresh
    white breadcrumbs
30 g (1 oz/⅓ cup) shaved
    parmesan cheese

Roast carrot with mint and red wine vinegar

Serves 6 as a side

INGREDIENTS

6–8 carrots, halved lengthways and thinly sliced

60 ml (2 fl oz/¼ cup) olive oil

1 teaspoon finely chopped garlic

2 tablespoons red wine vinegar

1 tablespoon torn fresh mint

METHOD

Preheat the oven to 200°C (400°F/Gas 6).

In a bowl, mix together the carrot, olive oil and garlic. Season with salt and pepper and toss well to coat. Transfer to a tray lined with baking paper and arrange the carrots in an even layer. Place the tray on the bottom rack of the oven and cook for about 10–15 minutes, or until just tender and starting to turn golden.

Once cooked, remove from the heat, place the carrots in a bowl and add the vinegar and mint. Toss well to combine and allow to cool to room temperature before serving.

This is a lovely salad to serve with grilled meat, or as a beautiful sandwich filling with any cold meats. For this recipe you will need a food processor with a shredder attachment or alternatively you could use a grater. You can substitute raw beetroot for the celeriac if you like.

Raw celeriac salad

Serves 4–6 as a side

METHOD

Cut the outside skin off the celeriac and discard, then cut the flesh into small pieces. Place into a food processor and shred them. Alternatively, cut them into smaller sections and grate them evenly.

To make the dressing, pour the olive oil, vinegar and lemon juice into a screwtop jar and shake well to combine. Set aside.

Place the shredded celeriac into a serving bowl with the capers and parsley. Pour over the dressing, season with salt and pepper and toss well to coat.

INGREDIENTS

1 small or ½ large celeriac
2 tablespoons small salted capers, rinsed and squeezed dry
1 tablespoon chopped flat-leaf (Italian) parsley

DRESSING

60 ml (2 fl oz/¼ cup) olive oil
1 tablespoon red wine vinegar
juice of 1 lemon

If using parsley from the garden, only use the young shoots from the centre — you will need about 3 handfuls of picked leaves. If you are buying parsley from the green grocer, then try to buy fresh young shoots as they will taste infinitely better than older stalks which will be woody and coarse on the palate. Wash and drain them well before using. This is a great salad to serve with fish.

Parsley salad

Serves 6 as a side

INGREDIENTS

2 bunches continental
    parsley, leaves picked
2–3 small cucumbers, diced
4 firm tomatoes, diced
1 small red onion, finely
    diced
2 tablespoons salted capers,
    rinsed and squeezed dry

DRESSING

60 ml (2 fl oz/¼ cup) olive
    oil
juice of 1 lemon
1 tablespoon red wine
    vinegar
4 anchovy fillets, very
    finely chopped

METHOD

In a large bowl, combine the parsley, cucumber, tomatoes, onion and capers and toss to combine.

Put the olive oil, lemon juice, red wine vinegar and anchovies in a jar with a screwtop lid and shake well to combine.

Pour the dressing over the salad ingredients, season to taste, and toss well to combine before serving.

Braised artichokes with peas and broad beans

Serves 6

Remove the tough outer leaves of the artichokes and trim the stems (in my family we peel and add the stems to the dish — cut them in half lengthways and then into small pieces). You will be left with the lighter coloured and tender heart of the artichoke. Place in a bowl of water with the lemon juice — this will prevent them from turning brown. Just before you start cooking, drain them well and thinly slice, removing the hairy chokes.

Heat the olive oil in a large frying pan over medium heat. Add the onion and cook for about 5 minutes, or until softened. Add the artichokes and cook for a further 5 minutes, then add the peas and broad beans. Reduce the heat to low and season with salt and pepper, to taste.

Finally, add 60 ml (2 fl oz/¼ cup) water, cover, and cook for about 20 minutes, or until the peas and broad beans have softened. If the vegetables start sticking to the base of the pan, add a touch of water and adjust the seasoning as needed.

When all of the vegetables are soft and starting to turn golden, remove from the heat, toss through the parsley and serve immediately. Braised artichokes go well with any meat dish or you can add cooked rice or pasta to the pan to turn it into a meal.

NOTE: Peas and broad beans are the only vegetables I use that are frozen, mainly because it is hard to get sweetness from garden grown ones — I leave these for eating straight from the bush.

6 young fresh artichokes
juice of two lemons
60 ml (2 fl oz/¼ cup) olive oil
1 brown onion, sliced
300 g (10½ oz/2 cups) fresh or frozen peas
300 g (10½ oz) fresh or frozen podded broad (fava) beans
1 tablespoon chopped flat-leaf (Italian) parsley

Pasta with broccoli sauce

Serves 6

INGREDIENTS

500 g (1 lb 2 oz) broccoli

2 tablespoons olive oil

60 g (2¼ oz) bacon, finely chopped

200 ml (7 fl oz) milk

500 g (1 lb 2 oz) pasta (I like orrechiette or shell shapes with this sauce)

60 g (2¼ oz/½ cup) finely grated parmesan cheese, plus extra, to serve

METHOD

Wash the broccoli and break into small florets. Boil the broccoli in a saucepan of lightly salted boiling water for about 12–15 minutes, or until soft. Remove the broccoli using a slotted spoon and reserve the water in the pan to cook the pasta in.

Heat the olive oil in a large frying pan over medium heat. Add the bacon and cook for 3–4 minutes, then add the broccoli, stir a little and pour in the milk. Cook for 15 minutes, stirring occasionally and breaking up the larger pieces of broccoli with a spoon — the sauce should be a milk green colour and quite thickened.

Cook the pasta in the saucepan of boiling water, according to the packet directions. Drain well, reserving a little of the water in a bowl, and return the pasta to the pan. Add the broccoli sauce and parmesan and stir well to combine, then season with salt and pepper. Stir in a spoonful or two of the reserved cooking water to give it a creamy texture. Divide between serving bowls and serve with the extra parmesan sprinkled on top.

Bullhorn are long slim capsicums (peppers), which I find are easier to cook with than regular capsicums and sweeter too. They are available in green, yellow or red varieties — a combination looks great on the table.

Roast capsicum with breadcrumbs and olives

Serves 6 as a side

METHOD

Preheat the oven to 180°C (350°F/Gas 4).

Cut the capsicums in half, remove the seeds and membrane and slice into strips. Place on a baking tray, pour over the olive oil, scatter over the garlic and season with salt and pepper. Cook for 30 minutes, stirring once or twice while cooking.

Remove from the oven, sprinkle over the breadcrumbs and olives, then return to the oven and cook for a further 10 minutes, or until the breadcrumbs start to turn brown.

Serve the roast capsicum hot or at room temperature with the parsley sprinkled on top. It goes well with with any grilled meats or as part of an antipasto platter.

INGREDIENTS

6 large red capsicums (peppers) or use 8-10 bullhorns, if available

125 ml (4 fl oz/½ cup) olive oil

1 teaspoon finely chopped garlic

30 g (1 oz/½ cup) fresh white breadcrumbs

90 g (3¼ oz/½ cup) green olives, pitted and roughly chopped

1 tablespoon finely chopped flat-leaf (Italian) parsley

Roast tomato, pancetta and mushroom soup

Serves 6

INGREDIENTS

- 2–3 kg (4 lb 8 oz–6 lb 12 oz) ripe tomatoes, blanched and skin removed
- 125 ml (4 fl oz/½ cup) olive oil
- 2 onions, thinly sliced
- 200 g (7 oz/1⅔ cups) diced pancetta or bacon
- 100 g (3½ oz) Swiss brown and field mushrooms, sliced
- 15 g (½ oz/⅔ cup) dried porcini mushrooms, soaked in water for 10 minutes, then drained (optional)
- 1 tablespoon finely chopped garlic
- 3–4 sprigs of thyme

METHOD

Use a sharp knife to score a cross in the top of each tomato and blanch in a saucepan of boiling water for 1 minute. Remove from the heat, drain well and allow to cool slightly before peeling off and discarding the skins. Cut the tomatoes into quarters.

Preheat the oven to 180°C (350°F/Gas 4). Line a baking tray with baking paper. Arrange the tomatoes in a single layer on the prepared tray and drizzle over 60 ml (2 fl oz/ ¼ cup) of the olive oil, season with salt and pepper and cook for 30 minutes.

Meanwhile, heat the remaining oil in a large saucepan over medium heat. Add the onion and pancetta and cook for about 10 minutes, stirring occasionally until golden. Add the fresh and porcini mushrooms, if using, then stir in the garlic and continue cooking for about 10 minutes, stirring occasionally. Reduce the heat to medium–low, add the tomatoes and thyme and cook for 10–15 minutes, stirring constantly. Add 1–1.5 litres (35–52 fl oz/4–6 cups) water to the pan and continue to cook gently for a further 30 minutes, or until thickened. Divide the soup between serving bowls and serve hot.

A girlfriend of mine, Amber gave this recipe to me many years ago and I think it is too good not to include here.

Tomato cake

Serves 8–10

INGREDIENTS

450 g (1 lb) firm, ripe round tomatoes
115 g (4 oz) unsalted butter
165 g (5¾ oz/¾ cup) caster (superfine) sugar
2 eggs
225 g (8 oz/1½ cups) self-raising flour
2 teaspoons mixed (pumpkin pie) spice
85 g (3 oz/½ cup) sultanas (golden raisins)

METHOD

Use a sharp knife to score a cross in the top of each tomato and blanch in a saucepan of boiling water for 1 minute. Remove from the heat, drain well and allow to cool slightly before peeling off and discarding the skins. Finely chop the flesh.

Preheat the oven to 170°C (325°F/Gas 3). Lightly grease a round 20 cm (8 inch) cake tin and line the base with baking paper.

In the bowl of an electric mixer fitted with a beater attachment, cream the butter and sugar until pale and fluffy. Add the eggs, one at a time, beating well between each addition. Add the flour, mixed spice, tomato and sultanas and fold all of the ingredients together until well combined. Spoon into the prepared tin and cook for 50–60 minutes, or until a skewer inserted into the centre of the cake comes out clean. Leave to cool in the tin for 10 minutes before turning out onto a wire rack. This cake is nice served warm or at room temperature.

Stuffed tomatoes

Serves 6

METHOD

Preheat the oven to 180°C (350°F/Gas 4). Line a baking tray with baking paper.

Finely dice two of the tomatoes and set aside. Cut a very thin slice from the bottom of each of the remaining twelve tomatoes so they sit flat. Cut around the tops with a small sharp knife and set the tops aside. Scoop out a heaped tablespoon of the flesh — try and keep the tomato firm. Reserve the flesh in a bowl. Arrange the tomatoes on the prepared tray and set aside.

Heat 60 ml (2 fl oz/¼ cup) of the olive oil in a frying pan over medium heat. Add the onion and cook for about 5 minutes, or until golden. Add the anchovies and cook for 3 minutes, then add the tomato flesh and reserved diced tomatoes and cook gently for 3 minutes. Turn off the heat and while the mixture is still hot, add the breadcrumbs, parsley and capers and mix well to combine. Season with salt and pepper, allow to cool, then stir through the parmesan cheese.

Spoon the stuffing into each tomato, gently but firmly pressing the mixture into the holes. Replace the lids, then drizzle with the remaining olive oil and bake for 45–60 minutes, or until they start to soften and turn golden. Serve with rice or couscous.

NOTE: A great way of using excess tomatoes is to cut them into quarters, drizzle with a little olive oil and season with salt and pepper. Arrange on a baking tray lined with baking paper, sprinkle over a little dried oregano or some fresh thyme and cook in the oven at the lowest possible setting for at least 12 hours, or overnight. Slow-roasted tomatoes can be stored for 3–4 days and are great to serve as part of an antipasto platter, with eggs or a simple roast.

INGREDIENTS

14 firm, ripe round tomatoes
125 ml (4 fl oz/½ cup) olive oil
1 red onion, finely chopped
6 anchovy fillets, finely chopped
90 g (3¼ oz/1½ cups) fresh white breadcrumbs
½ bunch flat-leaf (Italian) parsley, finely chopped
2 tablespoons small salted capers, rinsed and squeezed dry
35 g (1¼ oz/¼ cup) finely grated parmesan cheese, plus extra, to serve

Sicilian baked eggplant

Serves 6

METHOD

Preheat the oven to 180°C (350°F/Gas 4).

Lightly salt the eggplants and leave to stand for about 1 hour — this helps to remove any bitterness. When ready, place them on a clean tea towel to absorb any liquid and pat dry.

Heat 125 ml (4 fl oz/½ cup) of the olive oil in a large frying pan over medium heat. Add the eggplant slices, in batches, and cook until just brown on both sides, then remove to a baking tray and arrange in a single layer. Repeat with the remaining eggplant and oil until all cooked.

Heat the extra olive oil in a clean pan over medium heat. Add the onion and cook for 5 minutes, or until it starts to turn golden. Add the garlic and cook briefly, then add the tomatoes, season with salt and pepper, and continue cooking for about 5 minutes. Add 250 ml (9 fl oz/1 cup) water, then pour the tomato mixture over the eggplant in the tray.

Scatter over the parsley, parmesan cheese and breadcrumbs and adjust the seasoning as needed. Cover with foil and bake in the oven for about 30 minutes. Remove the foil and bake for a further 15 minutes, or until it starts to turn golden. Baked eggplant can be served as a main meal with rice or pasta.

INGREDIENTS

3 eggplants (aubergines), halved lengthways, then cut into three wedges

250 ml (9 fl oz/1 cup) olive oil, plus 60 ml (2 fl oz/ ¼ cup) extra, for cooking

1 small brown onion, diced

1 tablespoon garlic in oil (page 213)

1 x 400 g (14 oz) tin Italian chopped tomatoes

2 tablespoons chopped flat-leaf (Italian) parsley

70 g (2½ oz/½ cup) finely grated parmesan cheese

30 g (1 oz/½ cup) fresh white breadcrumbs

Italians often eat raw fennel at the end of a meal to aid digestion. It can be cooked in many different ways in soups, braises, salads or baked. It is in season from autumn to spring. Apparently it has a male and female version although some may dispute this. The male is supposedly round, sweeter and less stringy and the female is longer and flatter. I find that baby fennel, which is available all year round, is too strong and often tough, and avoid it for this reason.

Fennel and pea soup

Serves 6

INGREDIENTS

2 fennel bulbs

80 ml (2½ fl oz/⅓ cup) olive oil

1 onion, diced

300 g (10½ oz/2 cups) fresh or frozen peas

1 x 400 g (14 oz) tin Italian chopped tomatoes

METHOD

Remove the tough outer leaves from the fennel and discard. Remove the fronds and reserve separately. Wash and drain the fennel and cut into small pieces.

Heat the oil in a large saucepan over medium heat. Add the onion and fennel and cook for about 5 minutes, stirring constantly until softened. Add the peas and cook for a further 10 minutes, stirring constantly, then add the tomatoes, reserved fennel fronds and season with salt and pepper. Reduce the heat to low and cook for about 45 minutes, stirring now and again. If the mixture starts to dry out, add 125 ml (4 fl oz/½ cup) water.

When the vegetables are cooked, add enough water to make the soup to your liking. If you want a thick, hearty soup add about 1 litre (35 fl oz/4 cups); if you like more of a broth add about 1.5 litres (52 fl oz/6 cups). Adjust the seasoning, then bring to the boil and cook for a further 15 minutes. If you like, a cup of small pasta can be added at this stage for a more wholesome soup.

Sweet and sour onions

METHOD

Cook the onions in a saucepan of boiling salted water for about 10 minutes, or until soft — when tested with a skewer it should easily go through the centre. Drain well.

Heat the olive oil in a large frying pan over medium heat. Add the onions and cook for about 10–15 minutes, stirring often, until golden on all sides. Add the sugar and when it starts to caramelise, add the vinegar and cook for a further 5 minutes. Season with salt and pepper and serve hot. This is a lovely dish to accompany roast pork or lamb.

INGREDIENTS

1 kg (2 lb 4 oz) peeled small brown onions

125 ml (4 fl oz/½ cup) olive oil

55 g (2 oz/¼ cup) sugar

125 ml (4 fl oz/½ cup) white wine vinegar

Winter salad

Serves 6

INGREDIENTS

4 slices pancetta
1 fennel bulb, trimmed
4 spring onions (scallions),
   thinly sliced
1 small head radicchio,
   shredded
¼ head savoy cabbage,
   shredded
60 ml (2 fl oz/¼ cup) extra
   virgin olive oil
2–3 tablespoons red wine
   vinegar or lemon juice
2 tablespoons finely chopped
   flat-leaf (Italian) parsley

METHOD

Preheat the oven to 200°C (400°F/Gas 6). Place the pancetta on a baking tray and cook in the oven for about 5 minutes, turning once, until crisp. Remove from the oven, and when cool, break the pancetta into small pieces and set aside.

Remove the tough outer leaves from the fennel and discard. Remove the fronds and reserve separately. Wash and drain the fennel, then cut in half and slice as thinly as possible.

Put the fennel, spring onion, radicchio and cabbage into a large serving bowl and mix well. Add the olive oil, reserved fennel fronds, vinegar and parsley. Season with salt and black pepper and toss together. Top with the crispy pancetta before serving.

Oregano

Growing oregano is one of the easiest things to do in the garden. It grows almost like a weed. It is no comparison to the commercial oregano and is worthwhile planting your own so you can enjoy the fullness of flavour and aroma that it can add to a dish.

It should be picked when it just starts to flower. If you cut it at the base, it will reshoot each year, and if you are lucky you may get two crops from the one plant. Oregano is probably one of the few herbs that is better used dried than fresh. To dry it out simply pick the fresh herb, organise into bunches bound with kitchen string and hang it upside down in a covered veranda or in a garage until it dries, about 2 weeks. It can be left and stored as a bunch or crumbled and placed in an airtight jar. Once dry it can be stored and used indefinitely.

I think these days, with so many people choosing to be vegetarian or being gluten intolerant, that many recipes have become a little boring and unadventurous. This recipe is a great vegetarian alternative to a meat ragu or bolognese — the fennel sweetens the tomato and adds flavour. It's great served with any rice or pasta and can also be used as the filling for a lasagne, maybe adding slices of grilled eggplant (aubergine) or zucchini (courgette) between layers.

Tomato and fennel ragu

Serves 6

INGREDIENTS

60 ml (2 fl oz/¼ cup) olive
   oil
1 large white onion, diced
2 fennel bulbs, trimmed and
   diced
2 x 400 g (14 oz) tins
   Italian chopped tomatoes

METHOD

Heat the olive oil in a large saucepan over medium heat. Add the onion and cook for about 2 minutes, then add the fennel and continue cooking for 10–15 minutes, stirring constantly, until it starts to soften — it must be quite soft as you don't want the crunch of raw vegetables in your sauce.

Add the tomatoes to the pan, season well with salt and pepper, and continue cooking for a further 1 hour.

Serve the ragu spooned over your favourite cooked pasta or rice with a sprinkling of parmesan cheese.

Rolled pumpkin cake

Serves 6–8

Preheat the oven to 180°C (350°F/Gas 4). Lightly grease and line the base and sides of a 23 x 29 cm (9 x 11½ inch) lamington tin with baking paper.

Put the pumpkin into a saucepan and pour in enough cold water to cover. Bring to the boil and cook until tender. Drain well, then mash the pumpkin and set aside to cool to room temperature.

In a bowl, beat together the sugar and eggs until pale. Add the flour, mixed spice and cinnamon and stir well. Add the mashed pumpkin and stir gently to combine. Pour the mixture into the prepared tin and sprinkle the walnuts evenly over the top. Bake in the oven for 15 minutes, or until cooked through when tested with a skewer. Allow to cool in the tin.

Meanwhile, beat the cream cheese and honey together in an electric mixer for about 5 minutes until light and fluffy. When the cake is cool, turn it out onto a clean tea towel (dish cloth).

Spread the cream cheese mixture evenly over the top of the cake, leaving a 2 cm (¾ inch) border around the edges. Holding the tea towel along one of the longest sides, gently roll the cake to make a log — don't worry if it cracks a little as you roll, it adds to the rustic appearance and it will taste great anyway. Trim the edges neatly and dust with icing sugar before cutting into slices and serving.

250 g (9 oz/1⅔ cups) peeled, cubed butternut pumpkin (winter squash)
150 g (5½ oz/¾ cup) soft brown sugar
3 eggs
110 g (3¾ oz/¾ cup) wholemeal self-raising flour
1½ teaspoons mixed (pumpkin pie) spice
2 teaspoons ground cinnamon
115 g (4 oz/1 cup) walnuts, finely chopped
250 g (9 oz) cream cheese, softened
2 tablespoons honey
icing sugar (confectioners' sugar), to serve

meat and game

It's hard to improve upon locally grown produce for flavour. Knowing where food comes from is just as important as supporting small growers and breeders, while the variation between distinctive regional flavours makes for some great tasting meat. Central Victoria is fortunate to have an abundant availability of good meat and game, such as local Tuki lamb, Wessex saddleback pork, rabbits, quail, hare and venison. At the farm, Colin and I are able to access these products from local suppliers. We like to rear our own chickens, and find that most of the time we can feed ourselves and service the restaurant as well.

Chicken arrabiata

Serves 6

INGREDIENTS

2 tablespoons olive oil

1 organic chicken, cut into
    8 portions, or use
    6 chicken marylands
    (thigh and leg quarters)

1 onion, diced

100 g (3½ oz) thick sliced
    pancetta or bacon, diced

1 x 400 g (14½ oz) tin
    Italian chopped tomatoes

500 ml (17 fl oz/2 cups)
    chicken stock (page 112)

3 large or 6 small potatoes,
    cut into chunks

2 sprigs of rosemary

1 teaspoon chilli flakes

METHOD

Preheat the oven to 180°C (350°F/Gas 4).

Heat the olive oil in a frying pan over medium heat. Cook the chicken, in batches, turning until golden on all sides, then transfer to a baking tray. In the same pan, cook the onion until it just starts to caramelise and then remove to the tray with the chicken.

Add the pancetta to the pan and cook until it starts to brown, then add the tomatoes and cook for about 5 minutes. Transfer to the baking tray with the chicken and onion, then add the stock, potato, rosemary and chilli flakes; season with salt and pepper. Cover the tray tightly with foil. Bake in the oven for about 1¼ hours, then remove the foil and continue cooking for a further 15 minutes. Serve immediately.

NOTE: Any leftovers can be used to make a wonderful pasta dish. Shred the chicken meat from the bones, mix with remaining sauce and add to your favourite pasta.

Chestnuts are a great addition to braises instead of potatoes. In Italy they are also used to make cakes and desserts, but they are just as wonderful in savoury offerings. You can substitute the beef with lamb shanks, osso bucco or even duck, broken into portions.

Beef and chestnuts cooked in beer

Serves 6

METHOD

Preheat the oven to 170°C (325°F/Gas 3). Dust the beef with the flour to coat. Set aside.

Heat 60 ml (2 fl oz/¼ cup) of the olive oil in a large frying pan over medium heat. Add the beef, in batches, and brown on all sides, seasoning with salt and pepper as they cook. Remove to a baking dish once cooked and finish cooking the remainder. Set aside.

Heat the remaining olive oil in the pan over medium heat. Add the pancetta, brown quickly, then remove to the dish with the beef. Add the onion, carrot and celery and cook for about 10 minutes, or until transparent. Transfer to a roasting tin with the beef and pancetta. Pour in the stock, beer, orange zest, orange juice, and the drained chestnuts. Season with salt, pepper and nutmeg, to taste, and mix well. Seal the top of the tin with foil and cook in the oven for about 1½–2 hours, or until the meat is tender. Remove the foil and continue cooking for a further 30 minutes. Serve immediately.

NOTE: Dried chestnuts are available at delicatessens. If you want to use fresh chestnuts, slit the skin and boil them for about 5 minutes. You don't want to overcook them, just heat them so they are tender enough to peel. Add to the beef during the last 30 minutes of cooking.

INGREDIENTS

24 dried chestnuts (about 1 cup), soaked in water overnight, then drained (see note)

2 kg (4 lb 8 oz) chuck beef on the bone, cut into 6 cm (2½ inch) pieces

75 g (2¾ oz/½ cup) plain (all-purpose) flour

125 ml (4 fl oz/½ cup) olive oil

100 g (3½ oz) thick sliced pancetta or bacon, cut into small pieces

1 large onion, finely diced

1 carrot, finely diced

2 celery sticks, finely sliced

500 ml (17 fl oz/2 cups) beef stock or chicken stock (page 112)

500 ml (17 fl oz/2 cups) heavy malted beer

finely grated zest and juice of 1 orange

a pinch of nutmeg

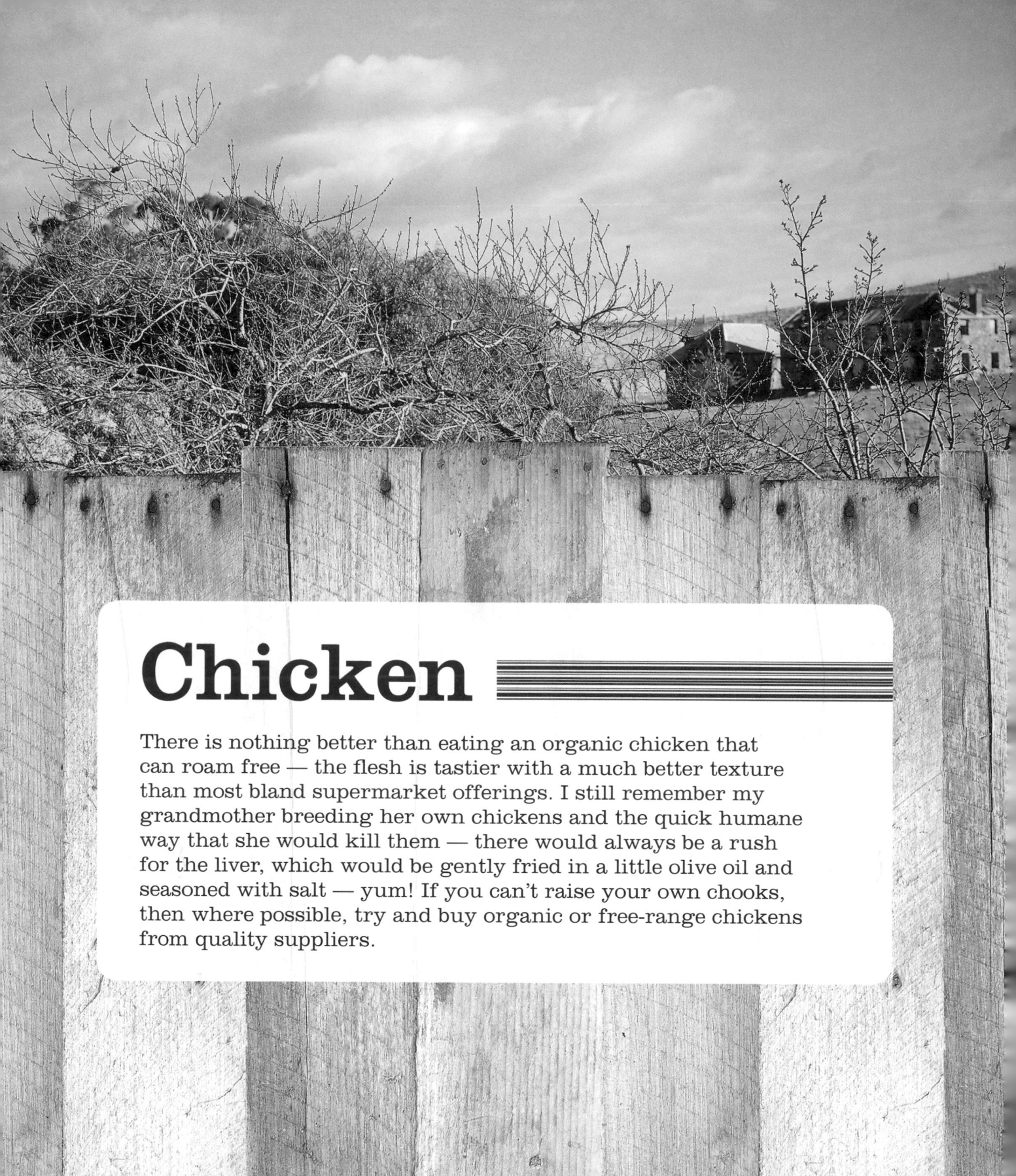

Chicken

There is nothing better than eating an organic chicken that can roam free — the flesh is tastier with a much better texture than most bland supermarket offerings. I still remember my grandmother breeding her own chickens and the quick humane way that she would kill them — there would always be a rush for the liver, which would be gently fried in a little olive oil and seasoned with salt — yum! If you can't raise your own chooks, then where possible, try and buy organic or free-range chickens from quality suppliers.

Citrus chicken

Serves 6

METHOD

In a large bowl, combine the olive oil, balsamic vinegar, oregano, garlic, thyme, chilli flakes, orange and lemon juice. Add the chicken, season with salt and pepper, and turn to coat the chicken. Leave to marinate overnight in the refrigerator.

Preheat the oven to 180°C (350°F/Gas 4). Place the chicken and marinade into a baking tray with the orange wedges and stock. Cover tightly with foil and cook for 1 hour, then remove the foil and continue cooking for a further 15–20 minutes. Remove the tray from the oven and remove the orange wedges to a plate to cool slightly. When they are cool enough to handle, squeeze the juice over the chicken and serve with couscous or rice. Potatoes can also be added to make a complete meal.

INGREDIENTS

60 ml (2 fl oz/¼ cup) olive oil

80 ml (2½ fl oz/⅓ cup) balsamic vinegar

1 tablespoon dried oregano

6 garlic cloves, crushed with the skin on

½ bunch thyme

1 teaspoon chilli flakes

juice of 2 oranges

juice of 2 lemons

1 organic or free-range chicken, cut into 6 pieces or use 6 marylands (leg and thigh quarters)

1 orange, cut into 6 wedges and seeds removed

250 ml (9 fl oz/1 cup) chicken stock (page 112)

Chicken stock

Makes about 3 litres (105 fl oz/12 cups)

INGREDIENTS

3 kg (6 lb 12 oz) chicken
  bones
2 celery sticks
2 carrots
2 onions, skins left on and
  halved
4 bay leaves
4 garlic cloves, skins left on
1 teaspoon whole black
  peppercorns

METHOD

Place all of the ingredients in a large saucepan or
stockpot and pour in enough cold water to cover. Bring
to the boil, then reduce the heat to low and simmer for
about 3 hours. Strain the stock and allow to cool.

Chicken stock can be stored in the refrigerator for
up to 4 days. I like to freeze it in batches so that I have
it readily available when needed.

There are times on the farm when we are inundated with wild hares. My nephew, Alex, hunts them for me and I use them to make this delicious ragu. I do prefer the young ones; unlike rabbit meat, hare meat is very dark — if you can't find hare, substitute with wild rabbit.

Hare ragu

Serves 6

INGREDIENTS

185 ml (6 fl oz/¾ cup) olive oil

1 large onion, diced

2 celery sticks, finely diced

1 carrot, finely diced

1 small hare, cut into 6 pieces (see note)

500 ml (17 fl oz/2 cups) red wine

2 x 400 g (14 oz) tins Italian chopped tomatoes

250 ml (9 fl oz/1 cup) chicken stock (page 112)

1 cinnamon stick

2–3 bay leaves

METHOD

Heat 90 ml (3 fl oz) of the olive oil in a large saucepan over medium heat. Add the onion, celery and carrot and cook until the onion softens.

Meanwhile, heat the remaining oil in a frying pan over high heat. Add the hare and turn to brown on all sides; seasoning with salt and pepper as it cooks.

Add the hare to the pan with the vegetables, then pour in the wine and cook for about 10–15 minutes over medium heat. Add the tomatoes, stock, cinnamon stick and bay leaves and season, to taste. Reduce the heat to low, cover, and simmer for about 1–1½ hours, stirring occasionally until the meat is cooked and pulls away from the bones easily. Take the hare pieces out of the sauce and remove the meat, discarding the bones. Return the meat to the sauce and stir well until heated through. Serve immediately with your favourite pasta or gnocchi as desired.

NOTE: Hare is available from some butchers and speciality meat shops — they will portion it for you.

In the fields and paddocks around our farm in Central Victoria we are blessed with an array of wild mushrooms to collect, such as pine, slippery jacks and field mushrooms. Collecting them is an adventure that we like to share with friends, but before you eat them you need to be 100 per cent sure of what variety they are; if in doubt don't eat them as some mushrooms can be poisonous. If you can't go mushrooming, just use a mixture of cultivated varieties.

Chicken with wild mushrooms

Serves 6

METHOD

Preheat the oven to 180°C (350°F/Gas 4).

Heat 60 ml (2 fl oz/¼ cup) of the olive oil in a frying pan over medium heat. Cook the chicken, in batches, turning until golden on all sides and seasoning with salt and pepper as they cook. Transfer to a baking tray once cooked and set aside.

Heat the remaining oil in the same pan over medium heat. Add the onion and cook until softened, then add the mushrooms and garlic; season with salt and pepper and cook until the mushrooms have softened — you may have to cook them in batches. Add to the chicken in the tray, then pour in the hot chicken stock with the thyme. Season well (I like a lot of pepper in this dish), then cover the tray with baking (parchment) paper and seal tightly under a layer of foil. Bake in the oven for 1½ hours, then remove the paper and foil and cook for a further 15–20 minutes to brown the chicken a little. Serve with couscous or rice if you wish.

INGREDIENTS

125 ml (4 fl oz/½ cup) olive oil

1 organic or free-range chicken, cut into 8 pieces or use 6 marylands (leg and thigh quarters)

1 large onion, diced

500 g (1 lb 2 oz) mixed mushrooms, stems removed and thickly sliced

1 teaspoon garlic in oil (page 213)

375 ml (13 fl oz/1½ cups) hot chicken stock (page 112)

2 thyme sprigs

Oxtail ragu

Serves 6

INGREDIENTS

60 ml (2 fl oz/¼ cup) olive oil

2 brown onions, diced

1 small carrot, finely diced

2 celery sticks, cut into
small pieces

2 oxtail, chopped into pieces

500 ml (17 fl oz/2 cups)
chicken stock (page 112)

3 x 400 g (14 oz) tins
Italian chopped tomatoes

2 tablespoons salted capers,
rinsed and squeezed dry

1 garlic clove, chopped

2 tablespoons chopped flat-
leaf (Italian) parsley

METHOD

Heat the olive oil in a large saucepan over medium heat. Add the onion, carrot and celery and cook for 5 minutes, then add the oxtail and turn to brown evenly on all sides. Increase the heat, add the stock and bring to the boil; cook until the stock reduces a little. Add the tomatoes, capers and garlic and season with salt and pepper. Cover and cook for about 1½ hours, stirring occasionally until the meat starts to fall off the bone. Alternatively, brown in a flameproof casserole, cover, and cook in a 160°C (315°F/Gas 2–3) oven for about 3 hours. When the meat is cooked, remove from the heat and set aside to cool slightly.

Remove the oxtail from the sauce and pick the meat from the bones, discarding the bones. Return the meat to the sauce and heat through for about 10 minutes. Serve with your favourite pasta or gnocchi, with the parsley sprinkled over the top, or simply serve the oxtail on the bone.

Lamb with potatoes and peas

Serves 6

METHOD

Preheat the oven to 160°C (315°F/Gas 2–3). Very lightly dust the lamb in the flour.

Heat 90 ml (3 fl oz) of the olive oil in a frying pan over high heat. Add the lamb, in batches, and cook until brown on all sides, seasoning with salt and pepper as it cooks. Transfer to a baking tray when done and discard the fat from the pan.

Heat the remaining oil in the same pan over medium heat. Add the onion and cook until soft and turning golden. Add the onion to the baking tray, then add the peas, potato and chicken stock and mix well; season with salt and pepper. Cover the tray with baking (parchment) paper and seal tightly under a layer of foil. Bake in the oven for about 3 hours, or until the meat is very tender — it should break up easily in your fingers.

NOTE: You can add 1 x 400 g (14 oz) tin Italian chopped tomatoes or 5 finely diced ripe tomatoes to this dish. Add them to the pan once the onion is cooked and cook for about 5 minutes before adding to the lamb.

INGREDIENTS

2 kg (4 lb 8 oz) boned lamb shoulder, trimmed and cut into chunks

150 g (5½ oz/1 cup) plain (all-purpose) flour

185 ml (6 fl oz/¾ cup) olive oil

2 brown onions, diced

250 g (9 oz/1 ⅔ cups) fresh or frozen peas, defrosted

3 potatoes, peeled and cut into quarters

750 ml (26 fl oz/3 cups) chicken stock (page 112)

Livers make a beautiful meal served with a simple green salad. Finely chopped, they can also be placed on top of some toasted bread and be eaten as a snack.

Chicken livers with Marsala and onions

Serves 6

INGREDIENTS

500 g (1 lb 2 oz) fresh chicken livers
80 ml (2½ fl oz/⅓ cup) olive oil
1 red onion, sliced
60 ml (2 fl oz/¼ cup) dry Marsala (see note)
1 tablespoon butter

METHOD

Clean the livers, removing any membrane, and cut each into two pieces.

Heat 2 tablespoons of the olive oil in a frying pan over medium heat. Add the onion and cook gently until translucent and starting to go brown, then remove to a plate.

Heat the remaining olive oil in the same pan over high heat. Add the livers and cook for about 5–10 minutes — the cooking time will depend on size of the livers and whether you like them pink or well done — season well with salt and pepper, turning the livers halfway through cooking. Reduce the heat to medium, return the onion to the pan, then add the Marsala and cook for a further 2 minutes. Reduce the heat to low, add the butter and cook just until the butter melts, then remove from the heat and serve immediately.

NOTE: It is important to use a dry Marsala and not a sweet one. Good Marsala, which comes from Italy, is available from most good bottle shops.

Rabbit with tomato and onions

Serves 6

METHOD

Cut the rabbit into pieces, removing and discarding the rib cage, as it will break up during cooking and leave too many small bones.

Heat 60 ml (2 floz/¼ cup) of the olive oil in a frying pan over medium heat. Add the rabbit and turn to brown all over, seasoning with salt and pepper as you cook. Set aside.

Heat the remaining oil in a saucepan that is large enough to hold the rabbit. Add the onion and cook over medium heat until quite soft and starting to caramelise. Add the tomatoes and cook for about 5 minutes, then season with salt and pepper and add the rabbit, rosemary and stock. Adjust the seasoning, reduce the heat to low, cover, and cook for about 30 minutes, stirring occasionally.

Add the potato to the pan and cook for a further 30 minutes. I find rabbit varies in tenderness depending on the time of year — when the meat falls from the bone it is ready. If not, cook for a little longer.

You can serve the rabbit with a fresh salad on the side. It also makes a lovely pasta sauce — just omit the potatoes and when cooked, remove the meat from the bone before returning to the sauce, then serve over your favourite pasta.

INGREDIENTS

2 wild rabbits
125 ml (4 fl oz/½ cup) olive oil
2 large onions, sliced
8 ripe tomatoes, peeled and chopped
1 rosemary sprig
250 ml (9 fl oz/1 cup) chicken stock (page 112) or water
3 potatoes, peeled and cut into quarters

Slow-cooked lamb shoulder

Serves 6

INGREDIENTS

125 ml (4 floz/½ cup) olive
   oil
2 tablespoons dried oregano
   leaves
2 tablespoons chopped flat-
   leaf (Italian) parsley
5 garlic cloves, crushed,
   skin left on
2–3 kg (4 lb 8 oz–6 lb 12 oz)
   lamb shoulder
500 ml (17 fl oz/2 cups)
   chicken stock (page 112)
juice of 4 lemons

METHOD

In a large bowl, combine the olive oil, oregano, parsley and garlic. Season with salt and pepper and add the lamb, rubbing the mixture all over to cover. Leave to marinate overnight in the refrigerator.

Preheat the oven to 170ºC (325ºF/Gas 3). Season the lamb again, transfer to a roasting tin with the marinade ingredients, then pour the combined stock and lemon juice over the lamb. Cover tightly with foil and bake in the oven for 3 hours. Remove the foil and continue baking for a further 30 minutes, or until the meat is very tender. Serve the lamb with the cooking juices poured over the top. It goes well with the chicory and potatoes on page 40.

NOTE: If you wish, you can add potatoes to this dish halfway through cooking — you will need about 4 potatoes, cut into quarters.

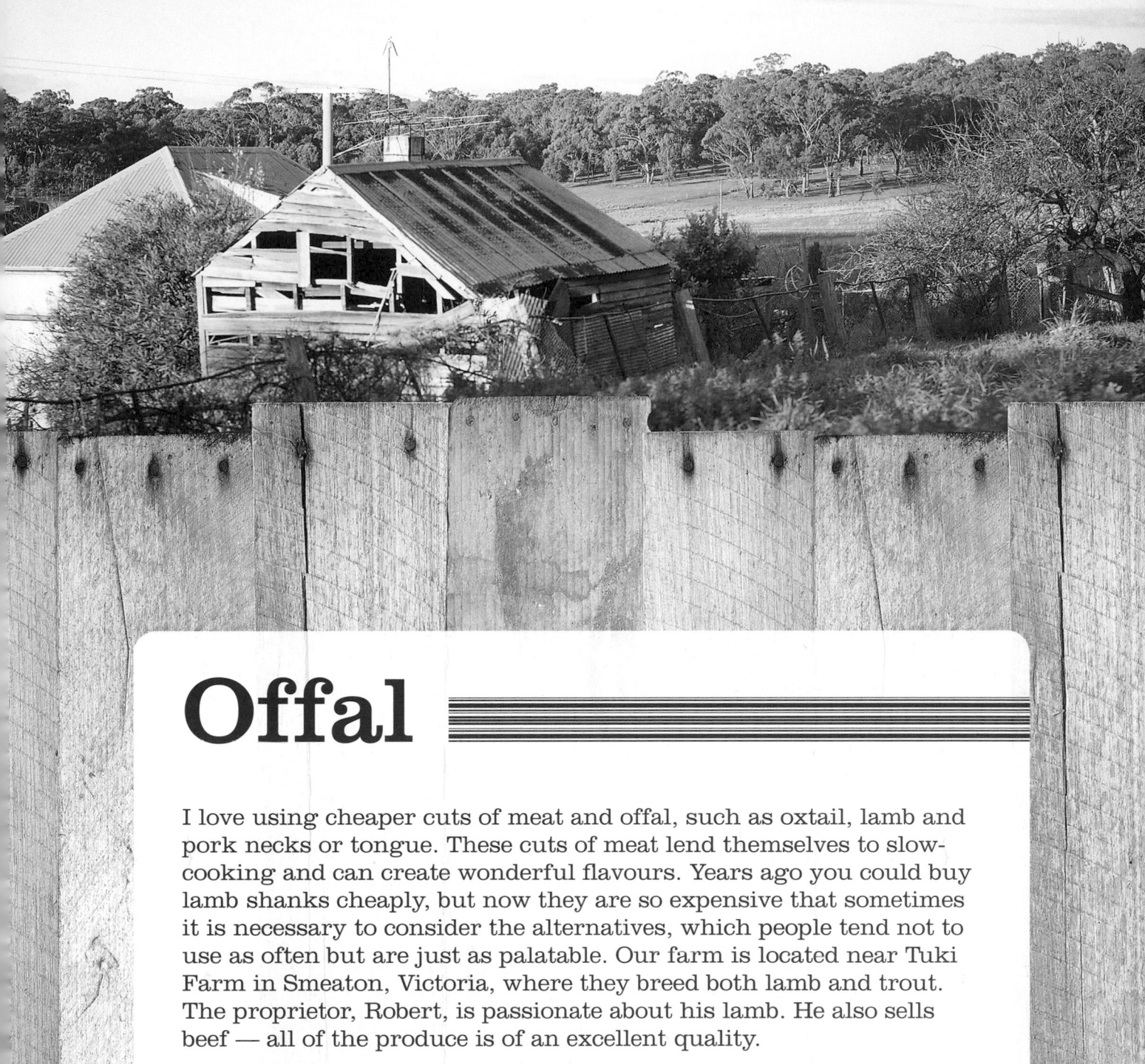

Offal

I love using cheaper cuts of meat and offal, such as oxtail, lamb and pork necks or tongue. These cuts of meat lend themselves to slow-cooking and can create wonderful flavours. Years ago you could buy lamb shanks cheaply, but now they are so expensive that sometimes it is necessary to consider the alternatives, which people tend not to use as often but are just as palatable. Our farm is located near Tuki Farm in Smeaton, Victoria, where they breed both lamb and trout. The proprietor, Robert, is passionate about his lamb. He also sells beef — all of the produce is of an excellent quality.

Tongues are always pickled when you purchase them. They need to be poached in a saucepan of boiling water before you add them to any recipe. Once poached and cooled they also taste great as a simple sandwich filling.

Tongue with potatoes and peas

Serves 6

METHOD

To poach the tongue, place the pickled tongue into a large saucepan with the carrot, celery and onion and bring to the boil. Reduce the heat to low and simmer gently for about 2 hours, or until tender. Take the tongue out of the water and when it is cool enough to handle, trim the tongues and peel them — if they are cooked enough they should peel quite easily (they must still be warm for easy peeling). Set aside to cool, discarding the vegetables and cooking liquid. Once cool, cut the tongue into 4 cm (1½ inch) chunks for the braise.

Preheat the oven to 180°C (350°F/Gas 4).

Heat the olive oil in a frying pan over medium heat. Add the onion and cook until translucent. Transfer to a large baking dish with the tongue, potato, peas, chilli flakes and stock. Season with salt and pepper and cover the dish tightly with foil. Cook in the oven for 1 hour. Serve hot with crusty bread on the side.

POACHED TONGUE

2 pickled ox tongues
1 carrot, cut into chunks
2 celery sticks
1 onion, cut into quarters

BRAISED TONGUE

60 ml (2 fl oz/¼ cup) olive oil
1 onion, thinly sliced
3 potatoes, peeled and cut into chunks
150 g (5½ oz/1 cup) fresh or frozen peas
1 teaspoon chilli flakes
750 ml (26 fl oz/3 cups) chicken stock (page 112)

Slow-cooked pork and fennel

Serves 6

INGREDIENTS

75 g (2¾ oz/½ cup) plain (all-purpose) flour

1½–2 kg (3 lb 5 oz–4 lb 8 oz) boned pork neck, cut into small pieces

125 ml (4 fl oz/½ cup) olive oil

1 large onion, peeled and chopped

1 large fennel, diced and fronds reserved

1 x 400 g (14 oz) tin Italian chopped tomatoes

1 teaspoon wild fennel seeds

500 ml (17 fl oz/2 cups) chicken stock (page 112) or water

3 potatoes, peeled and cut into 4–6 pieces

METHOD

Preheat the oven to 180°C (350°F/Gas 4). Place the flour in a bowl and season with salt and pepper. Lightly dust the pork in the flour to coat.

Heat 60 ml (2 fl oz/¼ cup) of the olive oil in a frying pan over medium heat. Add the pork and turn to cook until golden all over. Transfer to a baking tray.

Heat the remaining oil in the clean pan over medium heat. Add the onion and fennel and cook for 10 minutes. Add the tomatoes and fennel seeds, season with salt and pepper, and cook for a further 5 minutes.

Pour the fennel mixture over the pork in the tray. Add the stock, potato and reserved fennel fronds, keeping a little aside for sprinkling over at the end, then cover the tray with baking (parchment) paper and seal tightly under a layer of foil. Bake in the oven for 2½ hours, then remove the foil and baking paper and cook for a further 30 minutes, or until tender. Serve hot, sprinkled with the reserved fennel fronds.

NOTE: You can use lamb, beef or chicken marylands (leg and thigh quarters) instead of the pork in this dish. However, if you do use chicken, reduce the cooking time to 2 hours.

Slow-baked leg of lamb under salt

Serves 6–8

METHOD

Crush the fennel seeds using a mortar and pestle, pounding until fine. Add the garlic, parsley and olive oil and pound to make a paste; season with salt and pepper. Rub this mixture over the lamb leg to cover — you can marinate in the refrigerator overnight if you wish.

Preheat the oven to 150°C (300°F/Gas 2). Spread some of the rock salt to form a thin layer in the base of a large deep roasting tin.

Place the lamb in the roasting tin and cover with the vine leaves as tightly as possible. Pour the remaining rock salt over the lamb so that you have completely covered the meat and the bone. Spray lightly with water to seal the salt.

Bake the lamb in the oven for about 5 hours. To serve, gently remove the salt and discard the leaves — the lamb should be quite tender and smell amazing. Serve hot or at room temperature with a lovely salad. You can serve the cooked lamb with more of the fennel rub — you will need to make twice as much and set half aside. Add a little extra olive oil before drizzling over the top of the lamb.

NOTE: If you want to cook two legs together place them side by side in opposite directions, you will need a little more salt to cover.

INGREDIENTS

1 tablespoon wild fennel seeds

3 garlic cloves

1 large handful flat-leaf (Italian) parsley, leaves picked

125 ml (4 fl oz/½ cup) olive oil

2–3 kg (4 lb 8 oz–6 lb 12 oz) leg of lamb

3–4 kg (6 lb 12 oz–9 lb) rock salt (depending upon the size of your leg of lamb)

12–15 fresh grapevine leaves, blanched for about 3 minutes, then drained (or use pre-bought leaves, rinsed)

Bullboars

Yandoit's earliest Northern Italian settlers introduced their own rather unusual sausage to the region. Despite the fact the Italians closely guarded their recipes and referred to it only as 'sausage' it became widely embraced by the wider community and dubbed the Bullboar. Slow Food Australia has nominated the Bullboar as an Ark of Taste food. The Bullboar is half beef, half pork — it feels drier and denser than the pork sausages of my native Sicily, and the Northern Italian spices are totally foreign to me when used in this savoury manner.

The old Gervasoni recipe made an enormous number of sausages — in those times, a steer and a pig would be killed in June or July and combined for fresh and dried versions. 'Salt petre' (potassium nitrate) was also added as a preservative (and would keep them 'pinker' for longer). I think it makes a happier (and healthier) recipe to exclude the salt petre.

Ask your butcher to grind the meats for you, but they must be coarsely ground. This recipe makes 24 sausages that should be kept refrigerated and used within 2–3 days. Some people choose to use the mixture to make rissoles or patties and not have the extra work of filling the sausage skins.

Bullboars

Makes 2.8 kg (6 lb 4 oz) sausages

INGREDIENTS

1.2 kg (2 lb 8 oz) lean beef, coarsely ground

600 g (1 lb 5 oz) pork shoulder, coarsely ground

600 g (1 lb 5 oz) pork belly, skin removed, meat and fat coarsely ground

4 garlic cloves, finely chopped

300 ml (10½ fl oz) red wine

2½ teaspoons allspice

1¼ teaspoons ground cinnamon

1¼ tablespoons ground white pepper

1 teaspoon ground nutmeg

1 teaspoon ground cloves

40 g (1½ oz) salt

3 metres (10 feet) of 38 mm (1½ inch) sausage casing (see note)

METHOD

In large bowl, combine all of the ingredients, except the sausage casing, and use your hands to combine everything together. Cover with plastic wrap and refrigerate overnight.

The following day, rinse the sausage skins in plenty of fresh water. There are various ways of filling the skins, you can use a piston type filler, an attachment on your food processor or mincer, or even fill them by hand using a piping bag with a filling nozzle. To do this, slide the skins over the nozzle, pipe a little to exclude any air and tie off the end. Continue filling, then tying or twisting every 10 cm (4 inches) or so. The sausages should be firmly filled and about 3 cm (1¼ inch) wide.

For best results, the sausages should be poached in simmering water for 10 minutes before being barbecued or baked to your liking.

These sausages are great served with the winter salad on page 94.

NOTE: The casings for these traditional sausages are usually sold salted and are available from most butcher shops. You will need to soak them and rinse them two or three times to clear away any residual smell.

wild harvest

I like nothing better than to forage for wild food along country roadsides, railway lines and in beautiful pine forests. The pleasure of picking things directly from the source brings much satisfaction — I often think these foods taste better simply because they are natural and free. Forest and field mushrooms, wild fennel, chicory, rabe, cardoons (Scotch thistle), stinging nettles and watercress can all be found if you can spare the time to look. Pleasingly, a lot of these wild weeds are becoming increasingly popular at farmers' markets. On the farm we are lucky enough to get wild rabbit and hare, which make excellent eating. Rabbits used to be considered a poor man's meat but now they are quite expensive to buy, although there are so many on our property I can't imagine how this is justified!

Wild fennel can usually be found growing wild during late winter and early spring. Its flavour is much stronger than cultivated fennel bulbs. The fronds can be eaten, and when the fennel grows flowers in midsummer, the seeds can be picked and dried and add a wonderful flavour to a dish.

Wild fennel fritters

Serves 6

INGREDIENTS

2 bunches wild fennel
   (see note)
150 g (5½ oz/1 cup) self-
   raising flour
100 g (3½ oz/¾ cup)
   grated parmesan cheese
1 teaspoon garlic in oil
   (page 213)
2 tablespoons finely chopped
   flat-leaf (Italian) parsley
2 eggs, lightly beaten
125 ml (4 fl oz/½ cup) olive
   oil

METHOD

Wash the fennel in salted water to remove any dirt. Bring a saucepan of water to the boil. Add the fennel and cook until the stalks are tender — the cooking time will vary depending on how young and tender the fennel is. Drain well and when cool, finely chop the fennel and place in a large bowl.

Add the flour, cheese, garlic and parsley to the fennel and mix well to combine. Add the eggs, season with salt and pepper and stir well — if the mixture is too dry, add a little water; if it is too wet, add a little flour — it should be the consistency of a thick cake batter.

Heat enough oil to cover the base of a non-stick frying pan over medium heat. Add spoonfuls of the mixture to the pan, in batches, and cook until golden underneath. Turn over and flatten slightly with the back of a fork and continue cooking the other side until golden. Repeat with more oil and the remaining fritter mixture until all are cooked. Serve immediately.

NOTE: If you can't get your hands on any wild fennel, use regular fennel bulbs, cut into small dice. You will need to boil them until tender, drain well, and continue to follow the method steps above to make fennel fritters. It is also very nice to use a combination of the two.

Wild weeds

Wild weeds are my favourite things to eat — they have quite a strong taste and some can be quite bitter, but pan-fried with a little beaten egg and they become something quite spectacular. It is getting harder to collect wild weeds as the urban sprawl expands and councils become ever-more vigilant with their sprays. If you have a garden at home you probably have a few weeds between the vegetables – stinging nettles and purslane grow most places, although you can buy domestic seeds of some of these varieties from speciality grocery stores.

Prickly pears are an unusual fruit that grow wild all over Sicily and in some parts of Australia. Sometimes called cactus fruit or Indian fig, they are a refreshing fruit to have after a meal and a lot of restaurants in Italy feature them on the menu. They were introduced to Australia during colonisation and soon become a problem weed — most species are still considered a pest. Some fruit shops sell prickly pears, but be careful handling them. As their name suggests, they have very fine prickly hairs, which are painful and hard to see to remove. I simply use a knife and a fork to peel them, hold the middle of the fruit with a fork, cut off both ends with the knife, slice the skin across the middle, then gently peel the skin off and take out the fruit.

Prickly pear and prosciutto salad

Serves 6 as a side

INGREDIENTS

6 prickly pears

1 handful of rocket
(arugula) leaves

60 ml (2 fl oz/¼ cup) olive
oil

2 tablespoons red wine
vinegar

6 slices prosciutto

50 g (1¾ oz/½ cup)
shaved parmesan cheese

METHOD

Carefully peel the prickly pears and cut into thin slices. Place the pears and rocket into a serving bowl and drizzle over the combined olive oil and vinegar. Season with salt and pepper, to taste, and gently toss to combine. Just before serving, top with the prosciutto and sprinkle over the parmesan.

Mostarda is a fruit paste, much like quince paste, although in this case made from prickly pears. It can be eaten fresh as a paste or dried in the sun to make a leathery fruit treat.

Mostarda of prickly pear

Serves 6

METHOD

Place the prickly pears in a saucepan over a medium heat and cook, stirring constantly, until reduced by half. Strain through muslin (cheesecloth) and measure out the liquid in litres. For every 1 litre prickly pear juice add 1 tablespoon of cornflour and stir well until smooth — try to avoid lumps forming; if the mixture is still lumpy, strain through a fine sieve and return to a clean pan.

Cook the mixture over medium heat for 30 minutes, then stir through the cinnamon and nuts, if using. Pour out onto flat plates and allow to cool until set.

The mostarda is now ready to be eaten soft, which is how most Italians like it, but my mother lets it stand for 2 days, then cuts it into strips and leaves it in the sun until it dries like chewy fruit leather. It is great as a snack or to serve as part of a cheese plate.

INGREDIENTS

2–3 kg (4 lb 8 oz–6 lb 12 oz) prickly pears, skin removed and halved
cornflour (cornstarch)
a pinch of ground cinnamon
75 g (2¾ oz/½ cup) hazelnuts, toasted, skinned and crushed (optional)

Stinging nettles are usually found growing in most vegetable gardens, especially around tomato bushes. The leaves and stems are covered in fine hairs that can cause a painful sting, which is how they got their name. Once blanched they don't sting. You can use them to replace any recipe calling for spinach.

Nettle frittata

Serves 6

METHOD

Blanch the nettles in boiling salted water for about 5 minutes, then drain well.

Heat the olive oil in a large non-stick frying pan over medium heat. Add the nettles and garlic and cook for about 3–4 minutes, then season with salt and pepper. Spread the nettles evenly over the base of the pan — if it is too dry, add a little more olive oil so that it doesn't stick.

In a bowl, combine the egg and parmesan cheese, then gently pour evenly over the nettles. Reduce the heat to low and cook gently until it starts to set around the edge — I like to push the edges of the frittata into the centre so that the mixture cooks evenly.

You can finish cooking the frittata in two different ways. The easy option if your frying pan is ovenproof is to cook it in a 200°C (400°F/Gas 6) oven until just set on top. Alternatively, you can place a large plate on top of the pan and use it to flip the frittata, then slide back into the pan and cook the other side for about 2 minutes, or until set.

Frittata is great served at breakfast or as a light meal with a salad, but I like to eat it as a filling in a roll or sandwich with a slice of prosciutto and some lettuce.

NOTE: This basic cooking method can be used to make various frittatas. Try it with the pan-fried mixed mushrooms on page 159 or the chicory and potato on page 40.

INGREDIENTS

105 g (3¾ oz/3 cups) young tender nettle leaves

60 ml (2 fl oz/¼ cup) olive oil

½ teaspoon garlic in oil (page 213)

4 free-range or organic eggs, lightly beaten

35 g (1¼ oz/¼ cup) grated parmesan cheese

Wild weeds pie

Serves 6–8

DOUGH

30 g (1 oz) fresh yeast or
   1 tablespoon dried yeast
2 teaspoons sugar
700 g (1 lb 9 oz/4⅔ cups)
   unbleached plain (all-
   purpose) flour or Italian
   pizza flour
2–3 teaspoons salt
100 ml (3½ fl oz) olive oil

WILD WEED FILLING

1 bunch stinging nettles
1 bunch wild chicory
1 bunch Cavolicelli (a form
   of wild broccoli rabe)
125 ml (4 fl oz/½ cup)
   olive oil, plus extra, for
   greasing and brushing
1 red onion, finely diced
1 tablespoon garlic in oil
   (page 213)

METHOD

To make the dough, put the yeast in a bowl with 185 ml (6 fl oz/¾ cup) water and add the sugar. Stir until the yeast dissolves, then cover and leave in a warm place for 10–15 minutes, or until the yeast is frothy.

Sift the flour and salt into a large bowl and make a well in the centre. Pour in the yeast mixture, olive oil and another ¾ cup water and mix together until combined. Roll into a ball and place in a bowl with a clean wet tea towel (dish cloth) over the top. Leave in a warm place for 1½ hours, or until doubled in size.

Meanwhile, prepare the wild weed filling. Trim and chop the green leaves separately. Cook the weeds, in separate batches, in a saucepan of boiling salted water until tender. Drain well, then squeeze to extract any excess moisture. Place in a bowl and set aside.

Preheat the oven to 190°C (375°F/Gas 5). Lightly grease a large flat oven tray, about 30 x 40 cm (12 x 16 inch) or similar.

Heat the olive oil in a large frying pan over medium heat. Add the onion and cook until it just starts to caramelise. Add the garlic and cook for about 30 seconds, then add the combined greens, season with salt and pepper, and continue cooking for about 10 minutes. Remove from the heat and set aside.

Divide the dough in half. Roll out one half of the dough on a lightly floured work surface to make a rectangle to fit the tray, about 1 cm (½ inch) thick, using your fingers to spread the dough to the edges of the tray.

Spoon the greens evenly over the dough, leaving a 2.5 cm (1 inch) border around the edges. Roll out the remaining dough to make a rectangle large enough to make a 'lid' to cover the greens, about 1 cm (½ inch) thick. Place over the greens and pinch to seal the edges and enclose the filling, making sure there are no holes for the steam to escape. Brush the top with a little extra olive oil and bake in the oven for 1–1¼ hours, or until lightly golden. Remove from the oven and cool for at least 30 minutes before cutting and serving. This dish can be served hot or cold.

NOTE: If you can't find any wild weeds to use, substitute with 1 bunch each of broccoli rabe, silverbeet and chicory.

You can use any of your favourite mushrooms to make this recipe. I like to use wild pine mushrooms, field mushrooms and slippery jacks, but you can just as easily substitute store-bought oyster and Swiss brown mushrooms if you prefer.

Pan-fried mixed mushrooms

Serves 6 as a side

METHOD

Wipe the mushrooms gently with a damp cloth. I like to fry the mushrooms separately by variety as they have different cooking times and it also helps to preserve their individual earthy flavours. You may need extra oil as some mushroom varieties will absorb a lot of oil.

Heat a little of olive oil and butter in a frying pan over high heat. Whichever way you choose to cook the mushrooms — don't overcrowd the pan. Add one lot of mushrooms along with a little garlic and cook quickly, tossing the mushrooms when they start to brown and seasoning with salt and pepper. Remove to a bowl and repeat with more oil, butter, mushrooms and garlic until all are cooked.

These mushrooms make a great side dish served with chicken or duck. You can also toss them with your favourite pasta and some grated parmesan cheese, or use them to make a frittata (see page 153).

INGREDIENTS

500 g (1 lb 2 oz) mixed fresh mushrooms
125 ml (4 fl oz/½ cup) olive oil
1½ tablespoons butter
1 tablespoon garlic in oil (page 213)

Marinated pine mushroom

Serves 4–6 as a side

INGREDIENTS

500 g (1 lb 2 oz) firm pine mushrooms (see note)

125 ml (4 fl oz/½ cup) olive oil

juice of 3 lemons

1 tablespoon garlic in oil (page 213)

3 tablespoons finely chopped parsley

METHOD

Wipe the mushrooms gently with a damp cloth. Slice the mushrooms and place into a bowl with the olive oil and lemon juice. Set aside for about 30 minutes for the flavours to infuse.

Stir the garlic and parsley into the mushrooms, season with salt and pepper, and mix to combine before serving. This is a lovely dish to serve with any fish or chicken — it needs to be served on the day it is made.

NOTE: Pine mushrooms need to be very fresh when purchasing — if they are a little limp or discoloured then don't use. If collecting from the wild they should be eaten straight away. Button mushrooms can be substituted, but make sure you choose small firm, young ones.

Yabbies are freshwater crayfish that can grow to about 30 cm (12 inches) long, but more often than not they are caught smaller than this. They can be purchased from your local fishmonger. You can use prawns if yabbies are hard to come by.

Yabby pasta

Serves 6

METHOD

Cook the yabbies in a saucepan of boiling salted water for about 5 minutes. Remove from the heat and refresh immediately in iced water. Drain well and peel the yabbies. Set aside.

Heat 60 ml (2 fl oz/¼ cup) of the olive oil in a large frying pan over medium heat. Add the garlic and tomato and cook for about 3 minutes, stirring constantly. Toss in the yabbies and cook for a further 3 minutes, then add the parsley and chilli flakes, if using. Season with salt and pepper, then remove from the heat and set aside.

Meanwhile, cook the spaghetti in a saucepan of boiling salted water according to the packet directions. Drain well, then return the pasta to the pan. Add the yabbies to the pan and toss to heat through and combine. Drizzle with the remaining oil before serving.

NOTE: If using peeled raw prawns in this recipe, they don't require the first stage of cooking as the yabbies. Just add garlic and tomato sauce and cook for 3 minutes.

INGREDIENTS

3–4 kg (6 lb 12 oz–9 lb) yabbies or 500 g (1 lb 2 oz) peeled raw prawns
125 ml (4 fl oz/½ cup) olive oil
2 garlic cloves
2 firm ripe tomatoes, diced
2 tablespoons finely chopped flat-leaf (Italian) parsley
1 teaspoon chilli flakes, (optional)
500 g (1 lb 2 oz) spaghetti

Pickling is quite an easy process, but if the contents of the jar are exposed to the air they can become contaminated. If at any time the contents in the oil are bubbling, they have gone off and should not be consumed. To prevent this from happening, make sure the contents are always covered with olive oil — this acts as a preservative. Placing the jar in the fridge once it is opened is the safest storage option, but you need to return to room temperature before serving. I prefer to use small jars, as once opened you will need to consume the mushrooms soon after. You can use field mushrooms if pine mushrooms are unavailable.

Pickled pine mushrooms

Makes 6–10 jars

METHOD

Clean the mushrooms by wiping them gently with a damp cloth. Cut away the stems and any dark or damaged parts and slice thickly.

Put the vinegar, salt, thyme and 750 ml (26 fl oz/ 3 cups) water in large saucepan and bring to the boil. Add the mushrooms and boil for about 3 minutes. Remove the mushrooms using a slotted spoon and spread out evenly on a clean tea towel (dish cloth) to cool and dry, about 3–4 hours. Discard the cooking liquid.

Arrange enough sterilised airtight jars with screwtop lids on the bench. Fill each jar halfway full with mushrooms — avoid using your hands, use tongs instead, as this will help to prevent contaminating the mushrooms. Divide the bay leaves, thyme, garlic and chilli flakes between the jars. Pour in enough olive oil to fill each jar and leave to stand for 1 hour. Top up with more oil if needed and secure with a lid. Store in a cool place. Wait for at least 1 week before eating them.

PICKLED MUSHROOMS

2 kg (4 lb 8 oz) pine mushrooms
1.5 litres (52 fl oz/6 cups) white wine vinegar
60 g (2¼ oz) salt
5 thyme sprigs

FOR BOTTLING

10 bay leaves
5 thyme sprigs, halved
5 garlic cloves, halved
chilli flakes (optional)
olive oil, for filling

fruit and nuts

What has happened to fruit? It is sad to realise that fruit has lost much of its original flavour due to modern consumer demands preferring large uniform produce,that is easy to peel and preferably seedless. As a society we have become so used to having perfect looking fruit that we think 'real' fruit is unsightly and undesirable. Homegrown fruit may lack some of these homogenised characteristics but it tastes so much better! At the farm we grow white peaches, bananas, apples and bitter almonds. The old mulberry tree on the property provides us with berries for a few months each year and from this we make wine, tarts, jams or simply enjoy them straight from the tree as nature intended.

This almond tart makes a great base for many different fruit variations, such as white or yellow peaches or fresh mulberries. Cooked fruit also works well. Peeled and cored pears, cut into quarters, can be poached in equal amounts of water and sugar with a cinnamon stick until tender. When cooled to room temperature and drained, they can then be arranged over the tart base. You could also used drained tinned pears cooked in a little butter, sugar and Marsala. Other combinations include prunes (halved, then soaked in a little Vincotto), sour cherries or blood plums.

Almond and fruit tart

Serves 10

INGREDIENTS

1 x 380 g (13½ oz) disc of
    pastry (see page 201)
250 g (9 oz) butter, softened
250 g (9 oz) caster
    (superfine) sugar
4 eggs, cracked
    and lightly beaten
250 g (9 oz/2½ cups)
    ground almonds
50 g (1¾ oz/⅓ cup) plain
    (all-purpose) flour
fruit of your choice (you will
    need enough to cover
    the top of the tart leaving
    a gap between pieces)
50 g (1¾ oz/½ cup) flaked
    almonds

METHOD

Preheat the oven to 170ºC (325ºF/Gas 3). Lightly grease a 25 cm (10 inch) loose-bottomed tart tin, about 3 cm (1¼ inches) deep. Roll out the pastry on a lightly floured surface. Gently place the pastry in the tart tin and press lightly into the edges, then trim any excess and chill for 20 minutes. Line with foil or baking paper and weigh down with pastry weights, dry beans or lentils. Place in the oven and bake for about 10 minutes. Remove the foil and pastry weights, prick the base with a fork and cook for a further 5–7 minutes, or until light golden. Set aside to cool to room temperature.

Combine the butter and sugar in a food processor, then add the eggs, one at a time, until well combined. Add the ground almonds and flour and pulse until just combined. Spoon the mixture gently into the prepared tart base, spreading evenly.

Arrange the fruit over the almond filling, pressing down lightly so it buries a little into the mixture. Top with the flaked almonds and bake for about 1 hour, or until firm to touch in the centre.

Apple fritters

Serves 6

METHOD

Slice the apples into 5 mm (¼ inch) slices. Place the apples in a bowl with the sugar and grappa. Mix well and leave to stand for 1 hour.

In a separate bowl, mix together the flour, egg yolks, milk and oil until smooth. Place in the refrigerator for 1 hour.

Beat the egg whites until stiff, then fold through the chilled flour mixture to make a batter.

Fill a deep-fryer or large heavy-based saucepan one-third full with vegetable oil and heat to about 180°C (350°F), or until a cube of bread dropped in the oil browns in 15 seconds. Dip the apple slices into the batter to coat, then gently lower into the hot oil. Only do a few at a time. When golden on one side, turn over and cook the other side until golden, about 3–4 minutes. Remove with a slotted spoon and drain on paper towel. Repeat with the remaining apple slices and batter until all are cooked and golden.

To serve, place the apple on a serving plate, drizzle with honey, if using, and dust with a little icing sugar. Serve warm.

INGREDIENTS

4–5 apples, peeled, cored and left whole
55 g (2 oz/¼ cup) caster (superfine) sugar
2 tablespoons grappa or Marsala (or other spirit)
150 g (5½ oz/1 cup) plain (all-purpose) flour
2 eggs, separated
250 ml (9 fl oz/1 cup) milk
1 tablespoon extra virgin oil
vegetable oil, for deep-frying
honey, for drizzling (optional)
icing (confectioner's) sugar, for dusting

Baked peaches

Serves 6

INGREDIENTS

6 yellow peaches (clingstone are best for this recipe)

lemon juice, for rubbing

1 egg yolk

1 tablespoon sugar

60 ml (2 fl oz/¼ cup) Marsala (or other fortified wine)

60 g (2¼ oz) butter, softened

40 g (1½ oz/½ cup) crushed Amaretti biscuits

30 g (1 oz/¼ cup) roasted hazelnuts, crushed (see note)

2 tablespoons honey

METHOD

Cut the peaches in half and remove the stones. Scoop out a little of the flesh with a teaspoon, mash the flesh with a fork and set aside. Meanwhile, rub the cut peaches with a little lemon juice to prevent them from discolouring.

In a bowl, whisk together the egg yolk, sugar and a touch of salt until frothy. Fold in the pulp from the peaches, add the Marsala, 20 g (¾ oz) of the butter, the biscuits and hazelnuts. Mix well and place in the refrigerator for about 30 minutes.

Preheat the oven to 180°C (350°F/Gas 4).

Mix together the honey and remaining butter in a bowl. Use a pastry brush to brush the honey mixture onto the cut side of each peach, then place a small amount of the biscuit mixture in the centre. Arrange the peach halves on a baking tray, cut side up, and bake for 30–40 minutes, or until the peaches are tender and just changing colour. Serve warm with cream, ice cream or whipped honeyed ricotta (see page 194).

NOTE: To toast the hazelnuts, place them on a baking tray and cook them for about 5–7 minutes in a preheated 180°C (350°F/Gas 4) oven, until lightly golden. Remove from the oven, tip into a clean tea towel (dish cloth) and rub the nuts to remove the skins.

Apple and walnut cake

Serves 8–10

METHOD

Preheat the oven to 180°C (350°F/Gas 4). Line a 20 cm (8 inch) round cake tin with baking paper and lightly grease with oil spray.

Peel, core and cut the apples into small pieces. Place in a bowl with the sugar and set aside.

In a separate bowl, lightly mix together the flour, bicarbonate of soda, cinnamon, allspice and salt, then add the nuts.

Beat the egg into the cooled melted butter, add to the apple mixture and stir to combine. Add the flour mixture and mix well (this mixture will be quite heavy). Spoon the cake batter into the prepared tin and bake for 55–65 minutes, or until a skewer inserted into the centre of the cake comes out clean. Leave to cool in the tin for 10 minutes before turning out onto a wire rack to cool completely.

NOTE: You can also add 160 g (5½ oz/1 cup) chopped pitted dried dates to this recipe if you like. This cake is also lovely made individually and served hot with custard. Line and grease a 12 hole muffin tin and divide the mixture between the holes. You will only need to cook the small cakes for about 30 minutes, but check with a skewer to make sure they are cooked.

INGREDIENTS

2 apples
220 g (7¾ oz/1 cup) caster (superfine) sugar
225 g (8 oz/1½ cups) plain (all-purpose) flour
1 teaspoon bicarbonate of soda (baking soda)
1 teaspoon ground cinnamon
1 teaspoon allspice
½ teaspoon salt
125 g (4½ oz/1 cup) roughly chopped walnuts
1 egg
125 g (4½ oz) butter, melted and cooled

Blood plum cake

Serves 8–10

INGREDIENTS

150 g (5½ oz) butter

150 g (5½ oz) sugar

3 large eggs

75 g (2½ oz/½ cup) plain
(all-purpose) flour

1½ teaspoons baking
powder

150 g (5½ oz/1½ cups)
ground almonds

8–12 blood plums
(depending on size), cut
in half, stones removed

2 tablespoons soft brown
sugar

50 g (1¾ oz/½ cup) flaked
almonds

METHOD

Preheat the oven to 180°C (350°F/Gas 4). Lightly grease a 24 cm (9½ inch) springform cake tin and line the base with baking (parchment) paper.

In the bowl of an electric mixer, cream together the butter and sugar. Add the eggs, one at a time, until light and creamy. Add the flour, baking powder and ground almonds and mix on low speed until just combined.

Spoon the cake batter into the prepared tin. Arrange the plums, cut side down in a circle, starting around the edge and working towards the centre — push each plum about halfway into the batter.

Sprinkle the cake with the sugar and flaked almonds, and bake for 1 hour, or until a skewer inserted into the centre of the cake comes out clean. Leave the cake to cool in the tin for 10 minutes before turning out onto a wire rack to cool completely. Cut into slices and serve.

Fruit mince and pear pie

Serves 8–10

INGREDIENTS

2 large pears, peeled, cored
  and diced very small
850 g (1 lb 14 oz/2½ cups)
  good-quality fruit mince
2 teaspoons cornflour
  (cornstarch)

LARD PASTRY

375 g (13 oz/2½ cups) plain
  (all-purpose) flour
150 g (5½ oz) lard or
  shortening, chilled
30 g (1 oz) butter, chilled
½ teaspoon salt
90 ml (3 fl oz) iced water

GLAZE

60 ml (2 fl oz/¼ cup) milk
2 tablespoons caster
  (superfine) sugar

METHOD

To make the lard pastry, put the flour, lard, butter and salt into a food processor and process gently until the mixture resembles coarse breadcrumbs. Transfer to a bowl and add the iced water, a little at a time, to just bring the pastry together, mixing gently. Divide the pastry into two even-sized portions, wrap in plastic wrap, and refrigerate for 30 minutes.

Preheat the oven to 180°C (350°F/Gas 4). Lightly grease a 20–22 cm (8–8½ inch) pie dish or flan (tart) tin with oil spray. Roll out one portion of pastry to make a 28 cm (11¼ inch) circle and use it to line the base and side of the dish. Refrigerate while preparing the filling.

To make the filling, put the pear, fruit mince and cornflour into a bowl and mix well to combine. When ready, place the mixture into the prepared pastry shell.

Roll out the remaining pastry to make a circle with an 24 cm (9½ inch) diameter for the lid. Place on top of the pie, trim the edges and pinch to seal. Prick the top with a fork, brush with milk and sprinkle with the caster sugar. Alternatively, you can cut the pastry for the lid into strips and arrange them over the top of the filling in a striped lattice pattern.

Bake the pie in the oven for 45–50 minutes, or until the top is golden. Serve warm or at room temperature.

Chocolate and walnut cake

Serves 8–10

METHOD

Preheat the oven to 170°C (325°F/Gas 3). Line the base and side of a 22 cm (8½ inch) round cake tin with baking paper and grease well with oil spray.

In the bowl of an electric mixer, cream together the butter and sugar until light and fluffy. Add the egg yolks, one at a time, beating well after each addition. Add the chocolate, flour and walnuts and mix well.

In a bowl, beat the egg whites until soft peaks form, then fold gently into the cake mixture. Pour into the prepared tin and bake for 45 minutes, or until a skewer inserted into the centre of the cake comes out clean. Leave the cake to cool in the tin for 10 minutes before turning out onto a wire rack to cool completely. Dust with icing sugar, cut into slices and serve.

INGREDIENTS

225 g (8 oz) unsalted butter
220 g (7¾ oz/1 cup) caster (superfine) sugar
6 eggs, separated
190 g (6¾ oz/1½ cups) grated good-quality cooking chocolate
150 g (5½ oz/1 cup) plain (all-purpose) flour
190 g (6¾ oz/1½ cups) finely chopped walnuts
icing (confectioner's) sugar, for dusting

Chestnuts

Traditionally, chestnuts have had many uses in Italian cooking.
Because they grew wild, they were a free food that could be used
in soups, braises and roasts, or made into flour and used in biscuits
and cakes. These days, you can buy them already peeled, but why
take the fun out of preparing them yourself?

There is nothing better on a cold winter's night than roasted
chestnuts and a good glass of red. Preheat the oven to 190°C
(375°F/Gas 5). Use a small sharp knife to slit a cross on each
chestnut — be careful as the skins can be tough. Arrange on a
baking tray and roast for about 30–40 minutes depending on the
size of the chestnuts. Sampling them along the way is a good test
— the skin should peel away easily, they should be slightly golden
and crunchy on the outside and soft in the centre.

Although this recipe may seem a little indulgent and fiddly, it is well worth the effort. You can break up the chestnuts with a fork and serve as a dessert with vanilla ice cream — delicious! Peeled frozen chestnuts are available from speciality food stores if you can't find fresh.

Caramelised chestnuts

Serves 6

METHOD

Slit a cross in the skin of each chestnut, being careful as the skins may be tough. Place in a saucepan of boiling water for about 5–10 minutes, then drain. When cool enough to handle, peel the chestnuts and set aside.

Melt the butter in a frying pan over medium heat. Add the chestnuts, cover, and cook for about 10 minutes. Remove the lid, then add the honey and sage and continue cooking, stirring occasionally, until the honey starts to caramelise, about 5–7 minutes. Serve warm.

INGREDIENTS

500 g (1 lb 2 oz) chestnuts
80 g (2¾ oz) unsalted butter, chopped
115 g (4 oz/⅓ cup) honey
4 sage leaves

Pears baked with dates, Marsala and honey

Serves 6

INGREDIENTS

6 firm, ripe pears

50 g (1¾ oz) butter, cut into cubes

100 g (3½ oz/½ cup) soft brown sugar

250 ml (9 fl oz/1 cup) Marsala, Vincotto (page 218) or sherry

160 g (5½ oz/1 cup) pitted dried dates

145 g (5 oz) honey

METHOD

Preheat the oven to 170°C (325°F/Gas 3).

Cut the pears in half (I always leave the skin on), remove the cores and place on a baking tray, cut side down.

Put the butter and sugar in a saucepan and cook gently over medium heat until the sugar has dissolved. Add the Marsala and dates and cook for 3 minutes.

Pour the warm dates and syrup over the pears, drizzle honey evenly over the pears, then cover with a sheet of baking paper and seal with a sheet of foil. Bake in the oven for about 20 minutes. Remove the foil and baking paper and continue cooking for a further 10–15 minutes to reduce the sauce and brown the pears a little. Serve with ice cream, cream or mascarpone.

Quick fig dessert

Serves 6

6 large fresh ripe, firm figs

3 tablespoons honey

60 ml (2 fl oz/¼ cup) Marsala, Frangelico or Vincotto (page 218)

250 g (9 oz/1 cup) mascarpone

½ teaspoon ground cinnamon

25 g (1 oz/¼ cup) flaked almonds, toasted

METHOD

Make cuts in each fig as if to cut the fig into quarters lengthways, making sure you don't cut all the way through, leaving the base end intact. Place a fig in each individual serving bowl — and open it up slightly so that it looks like a flower.

Heat the honey in a small saucepan over medium heat, then add the Marsala and remove from the heat. Let it cool slightly.

Add a spoonful of mascarpone to the centre of each fig, then pour a little of the honey mixture over the top and sprinkle with the cinnamon and toasted almonds.

These figs are also delicious served with a good vanilla ice cream instead of the mascarpone.

Quinces are one of those wonderfully aromatic fruits that years ago people grew in their backyards, but have become somewhat more of a rarity these days. Not only are they good to use as a dessert, but it would have to be one of the prettiest trees in the garden. A bowl of quinces makes a beautiful perfume in a room.

Quinces baked with Marsala and honey

Serves 6

METHOD

Preheat the oven to 160°C (315°F/Gas 2–3). Wipe the quinces with a clean damp cloth. I don't peel the quinces, just cut out any blemishes and cut them into quarters. Squeeze the lemon into some water and place the quinces in as you cut them to prevent them discolouring.

Sprinkle the sugar in a baking tray, then scatter over the butter pieces. Arrange the quince in a single layer, cut side down, then drizzle over the honey, pour over the Marsala and add 125 ml (4 fl oz/½ cup) water. Place a piece of baking paper over the quinces, then cover tightly with a layer of foil to seal. Bake in the oven for 30 minutes, then check the quinces with a fork — when they are soft they are ready (I find different quinces take different times to cook).

When the quince is cooked, place in a shallow bowl and drizzle with the juices. You can serve the quince simply with ice cream or cream or use as the fruit base for the custard tart on page 195.

NOTE: This recipe can also be made with yellow peaches — cook them for 15 minutes covered, and then for a further 10 minutes uncovered.

INGREDIENTS

3 quinces

2 lemons

100 g (3½ oz/½ cup) soft brown sugar

3 tablespoons butter, cut into small, thin pieces

2 tablespoons honey

125 ml (4 fl oz/½ cup) Marsala or Vincotto (page 218)

Pear, chocolate and pistachio cake

Serves 10

METHOD

Preheat the oven to 180°C (350°F/Gas 4). Line a 24 cm (9½ inch) round cake tin with baking paper and lightly grease with oil spray.

Put the pistachios and chocolate into a food processor and process to a coarse consistency. Transfer to a bowl and set aside.

In the bowl of an electric mixer, cream together the butter and sugar. Add the eggs, one at a time, mixing well between each addition. Gently mix in the flour and baking powder until combined.

Add the butter mixture to the chocolate and pistachio mixture, along with the orange zest, Marsala and pears and fold through. Spoon into the prepared tin and bake in the oven for about 1 hour, or until a skewer inserted into the centre of the cake comes out clean. Leave the cake to cool in the tin for 10 minutes before turning out onto a wire rack to cool completely. Dust with icing sugar and cut into slices to serve.

INGREDIENTS

150 g (5½ oz/1 cup) pistachios

200 g (7 oz/1⅓ cups) chopped good-quality dark chocolate

150 g (5½ oz) butter, chopped

150 g (5½ oz/⅔ cup) caster (superfine) sugar

3 eggs

150 g (5½ oz/1 cup) plain (all-purpose) flour

1 teaspoon baking powder

finely grated zest of 1 orange

2 tablespoons Marsala, Frangelico, Strega or port

2 pears, peeled, cored and cut into small pieces

icing (confectioner's) sugar, for dusting

Fig and fennel biscuits

Makes 30

INGREDIENTS

200 g (7 oz) butter, softened

60 ml (2 fl oz/¼ cup) milk

100 g (3½ oz) caster
(superfine) sugar

300 g (10½ oz/2 cups)
plain (all-purpose) flour

300 g (10½ oz) finely
chopped dried figs

1 tablespoon fennel seeds

icing (confectioner's) sugar,
for dusting

METHOD

Preheat the oven to 180°C (350°F/Gas 4). Line two baking trays with baking paper.

In the bowl of an electric mixer, combine the butter, milk, sugar and flour to make a dough. Add the figs and fennel and mix gently to combine. Knead the mixture a little, then roll heaped tablespoons into balls, slightly smaller than a golf ball, and arrange them on the prepared trays. Flatten slightly with the back of a fork, then bake in the oven for 12–15 minutes, or until the biscuits are golden. Allow to cool slightly before transferring to a wire rack to cool completely. Dust with icing sugar to serve.

NOTE: You can substitute the figs with 200 g (7 oz/1½ cups) chopped pistachios and the finely grated zest of an orange. Alternatively, try them using dried pitted dates and macadamia nuts or chocolate and raw almonds.

Sour cherry and walnut cake

Serves 8–10

INGREDIENTS

2 eggs

220 g (7¾ oz/1 cup) caster (superfine) sugar

60 ml (2 fl oz/¼ cup) Marsala

150 g (5½ oz/1 cup) plain (all-purpose) flour

1 teaspoon baking powder

½ teaspoon salt

125 g (4½ oz/1 cup) chopped walnuts

360 g (12¾ oz/2 cups) drained pitted sour cherries

WHIPPED HONEYED RICOTTA

200 g (7 oz) fresh ricotta cheese

115 g (4 oz/⅓ cup) honey

a pinch of ground cinnamon

METHOD

Preheat the oven to 180°C (350°F/Gas 4). Line the base of a 22 cm (8½ inch) round cake tin with baking paper and lightly grease with oil spray.

In a bowl, beat together the eggs, sugar and Marsala until light.

In a separate bowl, combine the flour, baking powder, salt, walnuts and cherries. Pour in the egg mixture and fold to combine, then add the cherries and mix gently. Spoon into the prepared tin and bake in the oven for 1 hour 20 minutes, or until a skewer inserted into the centre of the cake comes out clean. Leave to cool in the tin for 10 minutes before turning out onto a wire rack to cool completely.

To make the whipped honeyed ricotta, combine the ricotta, honey and cinnamon in the bowl of an electric mixer fitted with a whisk attachment, and mix until light and creamy. Serve with the cake. Whipped honeyed ricotta is also great served with poached fruits.

If you are lucky to have your own peach tree this is one of the most beautiful tarts you can make.

White peach and custard tart

Serves 8–10

METHOD

Preheat the oven to 170°C (325°F/Gas 3). Lightly grease a 25 cm (10 inch) flan (tart) tin with oil spray. Roll out the pastry on a lightly floured surface. Gently place the pastry in the flan tin, press lightly into the edges and trim any excess. Refrigerate for 20 minutes.

Line the pastry base with foil or baking paper and weigh down with pastry weights, dry beans or lentils. Place in the oven and bake for about 10 minutes. Remove the foil and pastry weights, prick the base with a fork and cook for a further 5–7 minutes, or until light golden. Set aside to cool to room temperature.

Arrange the peach slices in an even layer in the pastry base, starting around the edge and working towards the centre.

In a bowl, whisk together the egg yolks, cream, sugar, cornflour and a pinch of salt. Gently pour over the peaches in the pastry shell.

Sit the flan tin on a baking tray, place in the centre of the oven and bake for about 30 minutes, or until the filling has set. Allow to cool to room temperature, cut into slices and serve.

NOTE: As an alternative to white peaches you can use yellow peaches, nectarines, cherries, mulberries, poached pears, wild blackberries or baked quince (see page 187).

INGREDIENTS

1 x 380 g (13½ oz) disc of pastry (see page 201)
4–5 white peaches, cut in half, stones removed, then cut into thin slices
5 egg yolks
250 ml (9 fl oz/1 cup) pouring (whipping) cream
110 g (3¾ oz/½ cup) caster (superfine) sugar
1 tablespoon cornflour (cornstarch)
a pinch of salt

Stocking the larder

Having a larder stocked with good homemade produce is satisfying on a few different levels. Having ready-made foods always on hand can make life so much easier when unexpected visitors arrive. Not only should you have basic stores, such as flour, sugar and salt that allow you to create pastry or bake a batch of biscuits, but you can also rely on a range of tasty sauces and preserves that have a long shelf life. Apart from anything else, it is also a great way of using up a glut of ripe fruit or vegetables to savour and enjoy for another day. My mother always has a jar of homemade goodies on hand to give to visitors as they leave.

This is a great pastry base to use for any sweet tarts and apart from the butter, can be made with a few simple ingredients from the store cupboard. This recipe makes enough pastry to make two 25 cm (10 inch) tarts. You should always blind bake your tart for a crisper base.

Sweet pastry

Makes 2 x 380 g (13½ oz) discs of pastry

METHOD

Place the icing sugar, butter and flour into a food processor and pulse gently until the mixture becomes coarse. Add the egg yolks and pulse quickly — feel the pastry, and if it comes together in your fingertips it is ready. If it does not, add a little iced water and pulse until it comes together.

Divide the pastry into equal halves and then flatten each into a disc. If you only need to use one portion, wrap the other in plastic wrap and freeze for up to 2 months. Otherwise, the pastry is ready to roll out and line your tart tins (see pages 168 and 195).

INGREDIENTS

125 g (4½ oz/1 cup) icing (confectioner's) sugar
220 g (7¾ oz) cold butter, cut into cubes
375 g (13 oz/2½ cups) plain (all-purpose) flour
2 egg yolks, chilled

Drying fennel seeds

Wild fennel can be found growing along country roads, on the sides of railway lines and on vacant blocks of land. In the spring we collect the young green shoots to add to soups, to make a beautiful pasta dish with sardines or we blanch them and pan-fry them simply with garlic and a couple of eggs to make a frittata.

Wild fennel is unlike cultivated fennel in that it has a very small bulb. For me the most important part of wild fennel is the seeds. The quality of store-bought fennel seeds is no comparison to drying your own if you can find the plants growing wild. In my family we add them to preserves, pasta sauces, braises and as the vital ingredient in our homemade sausages and salami. Fennel seeds are also said to have medicinal properties to aid upset stomachs — simply steep them in boiling water to make tea or just chew on some seeds.

In early summer the plant grows long stems with a yellow cluster of flowers that turn to seed. It is important to pick the seeds while they are still green and plump. Cut the flower part with a pair of scissors and wash them to remove any insects or dirt. Lay the flowers on a tray lined with paper and leave in the open air, but not in direct sunlight, for about 2 weeks (bringing them in at night). The seeds should fall out of the flowers when dried. Store them in an airtight container — they should last you until the next season.

If you have an abundance of homegrown tomatoes or have a chance to purchase good, ripe tomatoes you can make a beautiful sauce for pasta, which you can bottle and keep for up to a year. I won't give specific amounts as it will vary depending on how many tomatoes you have — use roughly 1 onion for every 2 kg (4 lb 8 oz) tomatoes. The best way I've found to sterlise jars or bottles is to clean them in a dishwasher with no detergent, or simply boil them.

Pasta sauce in a bottle

METHOD

Score a cross in the base of the tomatoes and blanch them in a saucepan of boiling water for about 1 minute — this will make for easy peeling. Peel and chop the tomatoes then place in a colander for about 30 minutes to drain off any excess liquid.

Heat the olive oil in a large saucepan or stockpot over medium heat. Add the onion and cook until soft and starting to caramelise. Add the tomatoes and basil and season with salt and pepper. Reduce the heat to low and cook slowly, stirring often, for about 1–1½ hours — you should have a beautiful thick sauce.

The sauce must be kept hot while bottling, so keep the sauce over low heat. Ladle the sauce into the jars (work carefully so as not to burn yourself) and seal with tight-fitting lids. My mother places a blanket in the bottom of a box or crate, arranges a layer of bottles over the top, folds over the blanket and repeats with more bottles until full. The idea is that the sauce keeps warm and comes to room temperature slowly. When totally cool, after about 3–4 days, take out and keep in a cool dark place. Simply add straight to your cooked hot pasta for a quick and easy meal.

NOTE: If you open a bottle and it bubbles do not use it. Never add meat to your preserved tomato sauce.

INGREDIENTS

fresh tomatoes
onions, diced
olive oil
fresh basil leaves

Preserving

Preserved foods are a wonderful way to use up an excess of fresh produce from the garden. Often vegetables will be ready for picking at the same time and it is hard to make use of them all. Just about any vegetables can be pickled — my favourites are green tomatoes, eggplant (aubergine), artichokes, asparagus, capsicums (peppers), fennel, green beans and, of course, olives. The recipe for green tomatoes on page 210 can be used for many different vegetables as long as they are cut thin, although you may have to extend the curing time for larger vegetables.

Preserving is an easy process, but if not done properly the ingredients can easily become contaminated if exposed to the air — one of the secrets is to always top up the oil in your jars with olive oil, this acts as a protective layer. If you find that once opened the contents of the jar are bubbling at any stage then they are off and should be discarded. Placing the jar in the refrigerator once it is opened is the safest option; bring to room temperature before serving.

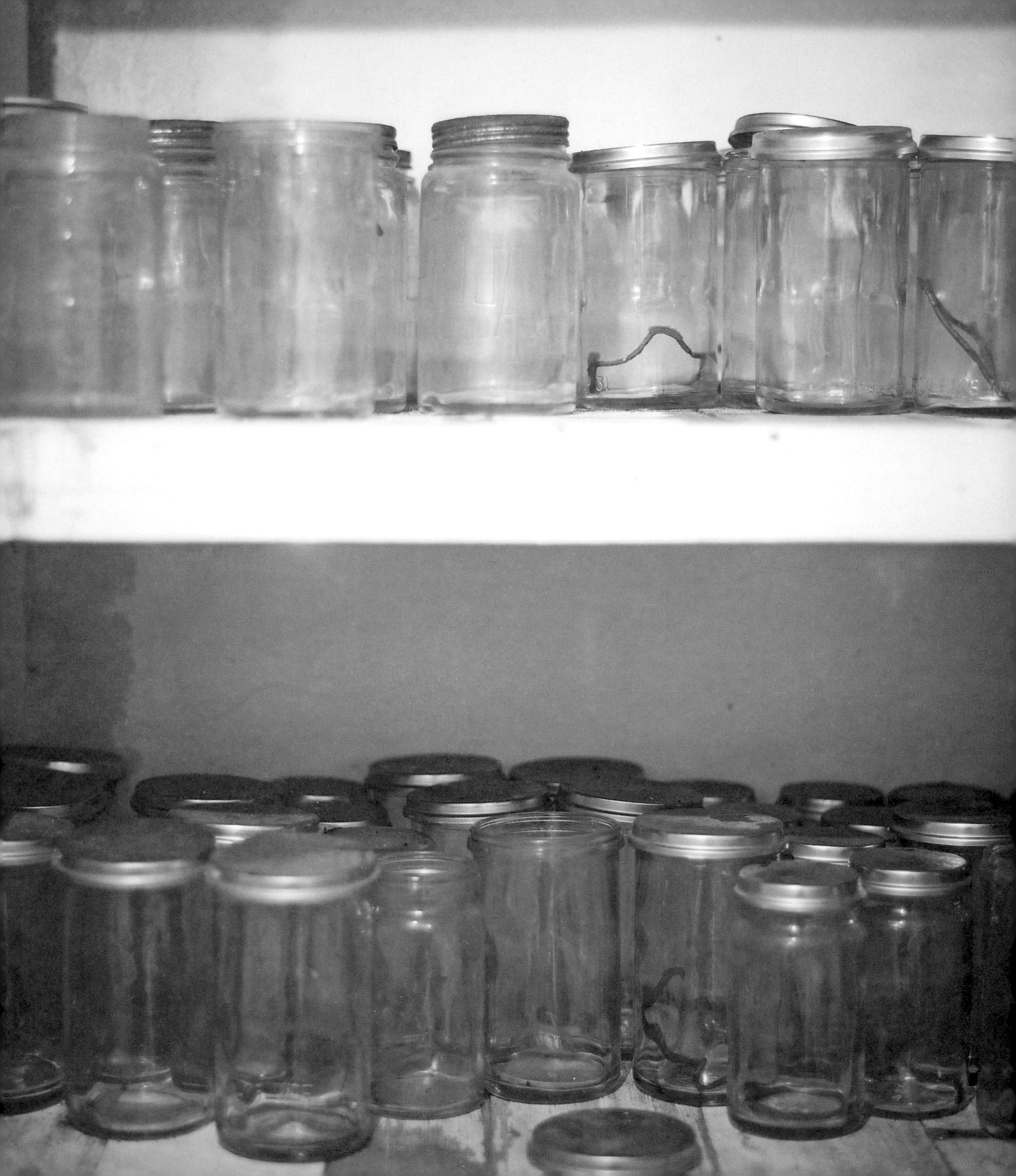

This is a great way to use the last of the tomatoes that don't ripen at the end of the season.

Preserved green tomatoes

Makes 4 large jars

INGREDIENTS

4 kg (9 lb) green tomatoes

240 g (8½ oz/1 cup) salt

1 litre (35 fl oz/4 cups) white wine vinegar

2 tablespoons fennel seeds

6 garlic cloves, peeled

2 heaped tablespoons dried oregano

6 fresh bay leaves

chilli flakes (optional)

olive oil

METHOD

Thinly slice the green tomatoes and place on a flat plastic tray. Sprinkle with the salt and leave to sit for 24 hours — the salt will turn into a liquid; give the tomatoes a gentle stir with a wooden spoon once or twice during this time.

Drain the tomato, place back in the tray, cover with the vinegar and leave to sit for a further 24 hours.

Drain the tomato and place in a bowl. In a separate bowl, mix together the fennel seeds, garlic, oregano, bay leaves and chilli flakes, if using. Pour in 250 ml (9 fl oz/ 1 cup) of oil, mix well and let stand for 2 hours. Place the tomato mixture into sterilised airtight jars and top up each jar with olive oil before sealing.

The jars can be stored for up to 1 year. Once opened make sure the tomatoes are always covered with oil, topping up as needed and store in the refrigerator.

Growing garlic in the garden is very rewarding, as not only do you have beautiful fresh garlic all year round which you know is totally organic and not a cheap imported product, but you can also use the young centre shoots of the growing garlic as an alternative to dry garlic. Add to soups, frittatas and pasta. This is a great way to keep chopped garlic in the fridge and use as you need it — I use it frequently in many recipes.

Garlic in oil

Makes about 250 ml (9 fl oz/1 cup)

METHOD

Place the garlic cloves in a food processor and process for a few seconds, scraping the sides and adding a little olive oil — you want the garlic to be chopped finely, but not ground to a paste. Place in an airtight container and pour over enough olive oil to cover. The garlic is now ready to refrigerate and use — top it up with oil as required and keep in the refrigerator for 1–2 weeks.

INGREDIENTS

2 heads of garlic, cloves separated and peeled
olive oil

This is a recipe written by Rene that I found in the old house on the farm — it is a great way of using up a glut of plums from the tree in the summer months when they are ready for picking. Plum sauce is a good alternative to tomato sauce — it can be added to gravy when you are having a roast and you can also use it to marinate meat or chicken before barbecuing, perhaps adding a little crushed garlic and chilli.

Plum sauce

Makes 10–12 medium-sized bottles

INGREDIENTS

3 kg (6 lb 12 oz) blood
    plums
1.5 kg (3 lb 5 oz/about
    8 cups) light brown
    sugar
1.5 litres (52 fl oz/6 cups)
    vinegar
1 teaspoon cayenne pepper
3¾ teaspoons white pepper
1¾ tablespoons allspice
3 cm (1¼ inch) piece
    ginger, well bruised

METHOD

Place all of the ingredients into a large saucepan over medium heat. Bring slowly to the boil, then reduce the heat to low and simmer keeping a close eye on the mixture as the ripeness of the fruit will determine the cooking time — when the stones are free from the fruit the sauce should be ready.

Strain the sauce, discarding the skin and stones, and allow to cool. Pour the sauce into sterilised jars or bottles with tight-fitting lids. The sauce is now ready to be used and can be stored for up to 1 year in a cool dry place. Refrigerate after opening.

Sweet tomato sauce

Makes 10–12 medium-sized jars or bottles

METHOD

Place all of the ingredients in a large saucepan or stockpot and bring to the boil. Reduce the heat to low and simmer, uncovered, for 3–4 hours, stirring occasionally until the sauce has thickened.

Pour the sauce into sterilised jars or bottles with tight-fitting lids. The sauce is now ready to be used and can be stored for up to 1 year in a cool dry place.

Serve the sauce as you would any tomato sauce (ketchup), with your favourite pies, sausage rolls, roast meats and sausages.

INGREDIENTS

4 kg (9 lb) very ripe
  tomatoes
125 g (4½ oz) onion, diced
750 g (1 lb 10 oz) apples,
  cored and cut into cubes
750 g (1 lb 10 oz) sugar
185 g (6½ oz/1¼ cups) salt
1 tablespoon cayenne pepper
2 teaspoons allspice
1 tablespoon ground cloves
65 g (2¼ oz) garlic, peeled
4.5 litres (160 fl oz) vinegar

Vincotto is a sweet wine made from the first pressing of grapes — it literally translates from the Italian as 'cooked wine'. You will also need vine ash from vine cuttings to prepare this traditional recipe.

Vincotto

INGREDIENTS

grape juice
vine ash
a strip of orange peel
a pinch of ground cinnamon

METHOD

Place the grape juice in a large saucepan along with the ash — you will need a handful, or about ¼ cup, for every 5 litres (175 fl oz) of grape juice. Cook over medium heat until it reduces by one-third. Remove from the heat and allow to cool for 24 hours.

Strain the liquid through muslin (cheesecloth), return to a clean pan over low heat and continue cooking until it reduces by half. Add the orange zest and cinnamon, leave to infuse until cool. Strain again and pour into sterilised bottles, allow to cool, then seal. Vincotto will keep indefinitely. It can be used to flavour cakes, can be baked with pears or simply poured over your favourite ice cream.

I found this recipe in Rene's papers when we were cleaning out the old house. Rene was famous for her mulberry wine. The mulberry tree on the property is quite old and has been hit by lightning at some stage. It produces the most delicious mulberries in mid to late summer, weather permitting. I only got to taste this once but I do remember it vividly as being quite delicious, much like a liqueur. Store-bought mulberries taste nothing like the real thing, so if you have room in the garden, plant a tree and enjoy the fruit. Blackberries can be substituted for mulberries.

Mulberry wine

METHOD

Put the mulberries, sugar, cream of tartar and 3.75 litres (130 fl oz) water into a large saucepan and bring to the boil for 15 minutes.

Strain into a large bowl, through a sieve lined with muslin (cheesecloth). Add the brandy, stir to combine, and pour into sterilised wine bottles, setting aside 60 ml (2 fl oz/¼ cup) in a separate bottle for topping up. Do not cork. Leave to ferment for 12 days — it can sometimes take a little longer. As it bubbles out of the top, add the reserved juice. Clean the neck of the bottles, cork them to seal and tie the cork down. The wine needs to be left for 8 weeks before consuming.

INGREDIENTS

3.5 kg (7 lb 14 oz)
   mulberries
2.5 kg (5 lb 8 oz) sugar
45 g (1¾ oz) cream of tartar
80 ml (2½ fl oz/⅓ cup)
   brandy

This candied orange peel makes a lovely addition to a topping for a cake or cheesecake, or can be chopped and added to a basic biscuit recipe.

Candied orange peel

METHOD

Peel the skins from the oranges leaving a little of the white pith on. Cut the peel into thin slices.

Bring a saucepan of water to the boil. Add the orange peel and when it comes back to the boil, continue boiling for a further 2 minutes. Drain. Repeat this boiling a further two times, using a fresh change of water each time.

Place the honey and orange peel in a saucepan and heat slowly until the orange peel is well coated with the honey, about 2 minutes.

Transfer the orange peel to a baking tray lined with baking paper and leave for 2 days or long enough for it to dry out a little bit and for the honey to set. Store in a sterilised airtight jar for up to 2 months.

INGREDIENTS

6 oranges
90 g (3¼ oz/¼ cup) honey

Index